MARRIAGE

—— ∞ ——

Love and Life in the Divine Plan

Leaders' Guide

Committee on Laity, Marriage, Family Life, and Youth
United States Conference of Catholic Bishops

United States Conference of Catholic Bishops
Washington, D.C.

Love and Life in the Divine Plan: Leader's Guide was developed as a resource by the Committee on Laity, Marriage, Family Life, and Youth of the United States Conference of Catholic Bishops (USCCB). It was reviewed by the committee chairman, Archbishop Roger L. Schwietz, OMI, and has been authorized for publication by the undersigned.

Msgr. David J. Malloy, STD
General Secretary, USCCB

CONTENTS

About the Cover

This image of the Wedding Feast at Cana, written by contemporary artist and iconographer Vladimir Grygorenko, depicts the major elements of the familiar story from the Gospel of John (2:1-11). At right, the head waiter tells the groom, seated beside the bride, that the good wine has been kept until last. The second man on the right represents the wedding guests, who do not understand the meaning of what has transpired. In the foreground, the server pours the water at Christ's command, and at left, Mary converses with Christ. This conversation shows forth Christ's desire to help the married couple at Mary's request, and it is central to the meaning of the piece.

PART I

INTRODUCTION TO THE GUIDE

A. Purpose of the Guide

In November 2009, the bishops approved a pastoral letter entitled *Marriage: Love and Life in the Divine Plan*. The letter brings together the Church's key teachings on marriage as a natural gift, as a sacrament, and as a public commitment between a man and a woman. It also discusses several contemporary challenges to marriage and how the Church addresses those challenges.

This *Leader's Guide* is directed to those who might serve as facilitators for reflection and discussion on the pastoral letter—priests, deacons, pastoral ministers, or small-group leaders. It was developed as a companion piece to help those who are married or engaged break open the text of the pastoral letter, reflect more deeply on seven key themes presented in the letter, and relate their reflection to lived experience.

Part I introduces the contents of the *Leader's Guide* and provides suggestions on how to use it, including a resource for facilitators and ideas on how to highlight marriage in the parish. Part II is divided into three sections:

- Background for Facilitators: Theological, pastoral, and spiritual information to help facilitators prepare for small and large group sessions.
- Breaking Open the Theme with the Group: A commentary on the theme with related references to *Marriage: Love and Life in the Divine Plan*, the *United States Catholic Catechism for Adults*, and the *Catechism of the Catholic Church*.
- Relationship to Lived Experience: A brief reflection followed by discussion and journaling questions.

Part III is a list of related resources and suggestions for prayer. The guide concludes with the full text of the pastoral letter, *Marriage: Love and Life in the Divine Plan*.

B. How to Use the Guide

The following are general suggestions on how to use the *Leader's Guide* effectively. While the guide offers specific suggestions on how to conduct reflection and discussion sessions, leaders should feel free to adapt its contents and recommendations to fit the scheduled format, length of time, and number of participants in a session.

- Read Part I, "Introduction to the Guide," and identify any recommendations to incorporate in your session planning. Review the resources and suggestions in Part III, and note which suggestions for highlighting marriage in the parish will reinforce and promote both the pastoral letter and reflection on the letter.
- Let the facilitator's guide be a roadmap for planning and leading these sessions. The steps are detailed and easy to follow; they cover everything from start to finish.
- Determine how to structure your particular session(s), using the sample session schedules as a starting point.
- Adapt the facilitator's guide and sample session schedules as needed to create a fruitful and comfortable experience for the participants.
- Provide, or request that participants bring, a journal or blank book for each session.

Reflection, Discussion, and Journaling Suggestions

The guide provides three different models for connecting the theme to the participants' real-life experience.

- "Reflection": Each theme includes a story that relates the theme to the lived experience of a married couple. This section can be used as a transition from reading or listening to the theme explanation to discussion. Invite the participants to read this reflection silently or aloud to the whole group, or have each couple read it together. Encourage participants to share any thoughts, experiences, questions, or insights that the story raises.
- "Discussion Questions": Each theme has three to five discussion questions, which may be used in large or small groups. With small groups, ask each group to identify a spokesperson and, after sufficient time, share a summary of the small group's conversation with the large group. Consider using newsprint, a blackboard, or a whiteboard to capture key ideas from the discussion.
- "Journaling Questions": Each theme has three or four journaling questions. Most of the following options can start during the group session, but they are best completed after the session is over or between sessions. Some options for journaling include the following:
  — If time is limited, read each journaling question aloud, pausing briefly so that participants can write down initial impressions or thoughts. Encourage them to return to their journaling in greater depth after the session is over.
  — Have participants rewrite the questions in a journal during the session. The rewriting process often functions as an opportunity to begin reflection on the question. Ask them to jot down just any *initial* words, phrases, or ideas that come to mind. Request that they refrain from writing a longer, more complete answer at this point. Invite them to choose a time or two before the next session to revisit the question and their initial responses. Encourage them to respond more

completely to the question in the interim, and prompt them to share their responses with their spouses.

— Using individual journals, ask the spouses to select one question for reflection. Invite them to commit to journaling on it each day for a week or until the next session. Encourage them to share their reflections, including something that they learned about their spouses and their marriages.

— Using one journal, ask one spouse to copy the questions on a right-hand page. On the next right-hand page, invite that spouse to respond. When these steps are complete, ask the spouse who responded to paperclip the question page and the answer page together and then invite the other spouse to respond to the same question on the left-hand page. Encourage the spouses to read each other's responses and to note their joint reflection on the next right-hand page.

Leader's Guide—and More—Available Online

The complete contents of the *Leader's Guide* are available for downloading at *www.usccb. org/loveandlife*.

You can use the downloadable files in two key ways: planning your sessions and creating handouts for your participants.

Make copies of the appropriate sections of this Introduction for other members of your planning team to help guide your decision-making process. Provide samples of the sessions and the resources to other team members who will be responsible for planning prayer or leading small groups.

The downloadable files also serve as ready-made handouts to copy and distribute to the session participants. For example, provide each participant with a handout for each individual theme, or give participants a copy of the list of Vatican, papal, and USCCB documents provided in Part III.

The Web site also includes links to other resources that further explore the themes of the pastoral letter. Visit *www.usccb.org/loveandlife* for additional information.

C. FACILITATOR'S GUIDE

Facilitator's Responsibilities

Congratulations! The pastor, a committee, or some local organization has invited you to facilitate a session on the pastoral letter *Marriage: Love and Life in the Divine Plan*. The following is a list of general responsibilities for a session facilitator, from preparation to activities during the session itself. Whenever possible, delegate specific leadership opportunities, such as leading music or facilitating a small group, to other individuals or couples.

- Coordinate the time and place of the session with the host. The "host" might be the parish, a committee or group within the parish, or a married or engaged couple.
- Plan an opening and closing prayer.
- Coordinate set-up of the space, including all materials needed.
- At the beginning of the session, explain its purpose, format, and structure. This information is provided in this first part of the *Leader's Guide*.
- During each session, give an overview of the theme (or themes) to be explored during the session.
- Establish small groups, if needed, and designate a small-group leader.
- If appropriate, invite and address questions, comments, or insights from previous sessions.
- Prepare and lead the presentation of the theme, or designate one or more members of the group to do so. The sections in Part II entitled "Background for the Facilitator" and "Breaking Open the Theme with the Group" provide material for a presentation. You should feel free to use additional material from the *Catechism* and the pastoral letter on marriage.

What Is the Host Expected to Do?

- Meet and work with the facilitator.

- Identify and reserve the space. Suitable space might include someone's home or a room in the parish rectory, offices, or school.

- Make sure there are enough chairs and tables, and set them up.

- Welcome the participants and facilitator.

- Provide or coordinate refreshments.

- Coordinate clean-up of the space after the session.

- Facilitate large-group discussion questions or the sharing of summaries of small-group conversations.
- Encourage the participants to make connections between their lived experience of marriage and the Church's teachings on and support for marriage.
- Provide instructions on and lead journaling activity.
- Close each session with a summary of the comments and insights that have been shared.
- Prepare and lead the session evaluation.
- Review and provide a summary of the evaluations to the host or other sponsoring organization.

Facilitating a Session

Materials Needed

- Marriage *Leader's Guide*—copies for the facilitator and any other large group leader
- "Relationship to Lived Experience" sections* for each theme—one copy per participant
- "Reference Resources" sections*—one copy per participant, or copies as needed
- Pens/pencils—one per participant
- Prayer aid—one copy per participant
- Evaluation form—one copy per participant
- Prayer table
- Cloth to cover prayer table
- Bible—New American translation, if possible
- Candle and lighter/matches
- Cross or crucifix
- Tables (2) for staging materials and distributing refreshments
- Chairs—one per participant
- *United States Catholic Catechism for Adults* (USCCA)—one copy
- *Catechism of the Catholic Church* (CCC)—one copy

> *These pages are available to download from *www.usccb.org/loveandlife*. Parishes and schools have permission to reproduce the downloadable PDF versions for free distribution.

Optional

- Name tags and markers
- Schedule (for multiple-evening sessions and weekend retreats)
- *Marriage: Love and Life in the Divine Plan*—one copy per couple or small group
- Journal—one per participant
- Music editions—one per participant
- CD player or MP3 player
- Music source (e.g., MP3s or CDs)
- Pad of newsprint; or blackboard; or whiteboard and markers

- *Rite of Marriage* or copies of marriage preparation booklets that include readings and prayers for the Sacrament of Matrimony
- *Catholic Household Blessings and Prayers*—one copy

Preparation

- Meet with the host to
  - Confirm the start and end times for the session.
  - Determine when to arrive in order to set-up the site.
  - Identify any space-related issues that you need to be aware of, e.g., whether candles can be lit in the room.
  - Clarify any materials or supplies, including food or drinks, that the host will be expected to provide.
  - Identify what materials are already available in the space, e.g., music aids, Bibles, prayer materials.
- Visit the reserved site beforehand, and decide how the seating should be arranged.
- Review the list of resources in Part III, and identify any that the participants should read beforehand and/or bring to the session. Copies of the resource list may be downloaded from *www.usccb.org/loveandlife*. Because the "Breaking Open the Theme with the Group" section for each theme draws specifically on the *United States Catholic Catechism for Adults* and the *Catechism of the Catholic Church*, make sure that copies of these two books are available to the participants before and during the session(s) as possible references. Copies of these publications and others listed in the resource section can be purchased from the USCCB (*www.usccbpublishing.org*) or your local bookstore.
- Review the "Background for Facilitators" section for each theme in preparation for the session(s) and the related passages in the pastoral letter, USCCA, and CCC. Material from all these sources is intended to help the facilitator better understand the theme by giving it additional context. It is not necessary to present

this material to the group, although facilitators may wish to mention one or more points when introducing the theme. (Downloadable versions of the "Background for Facilitators" can be found at *www.usccb.org/loveandlife*.)

- Plan an opening prayer and a closing prayer.
  - Prayer should begin and end with the Sign of the Cross.
  - Include a reading and reflection on Sacred Scripture in each prayer. Use any of the Scripture references cited in Part II for the seven themes, or use readings from the Rite of Marriage.
  - Select a song for everyone to sing together, or choose music to play in the background that will help participants reflect on or respond to the reading. Use the liturgical or scriptural indices at the front or back of the music edition to find appropriately themed liturgical songs. When using popular music, review the lyrics thoroughly to ensure that they support and communicate the Church's teaching.
  - Invite other leaders or participants to take a role in the prayer—e.g., lead the prayer, proclaim the Scriptures, or sing or play music. Give readers a copy of the reading in advance, or at least a citation for them to find the reading. Do the same with musicians—provide at least a list of the music.
  - Make a prayer aid, or delegate this task to someone else, if needed.
  - Before the session begins, cue recorded music to the start of the song.
  - Consider including a blessing or ritual as part of the closing prayer. See Part III for suggested blessings under "Prayers and Blessings."
  - For multiple evenings and weekend retreats, use the Liturgy of the Hours, part of the Church's Tradition, as a source for prayer, especially Night Prayer or Compline.
- Decide how you want to present the "Breaking Open the Theme with the Group" section for each theme. Options for presenting the theme include the following.
  - Invite other leaders to present the theme. Provide them with advance copies so they

can prepare. (Downloadable versions of the texts can be found at *www.usccb.org/loveandlife*.)
  - Prepare a verbal presentation to be given in large or small groups. Use the downloadable resources at *www.usccb.org/loveandlife* as a resource.
  - Prepare a few bullet points to present, or plan to use the PowerPoint presentation found at *www.usccb.org/loveandlife*.
  - Read the "Breaking Open the Theme with the Group" section aloud. Alternatively, provide the participants with the text ahead of time, and ask them to read it before the session or during a brief period of silence at the beginning of the session.

- If you have ground rules or basic principles for how you facilitate a group (e.g., confidentiality), write them down and present them during the welcome and introduction.
- Decide whether discussion in small groups or in the large group will be the most effective method for participants to process the "Relationship to Lived Experience" section. Unless the group is small (six people or fewer), consider varying the group size, e.g., large group for the "Reflection" sharing, small group for the discussion questions, and individuals or couples for the journaling.
- Decide what method of journaling will be used for this session. See the previous section for suggestions on journaling.
- Create a written evaluation form that addresses the following questions. Adapt the questions to fit the specific needs of your group.
  - Include questions concerning the setting. (Ask these questions after the first session of a multi-session format as well as on the evaluation form at the conclusion of the session.)
    - o Could the facilitator and any other leaders be seen and heard?
    - o Was the room set-up helpful in promoting active participation, discussion, and reflection?
  - Include questions concerning how the material was understood.
    - o Were the participants' expectations of the session(s) met? Why? Why not?

- What did participants take away from the session(s)?
  - What did they find helpful? Not helpful?
  - How could the presentations, discussion, or journaling be improved?
- — Include questions to determine what follow-up needs to take place.
  - What could the parish (or other sponsoring organization) do to support further discussion and reflection on the marriage pastoral letter?
  - Would you be interested in another program like this if it were available? What topics might interest you?
  - Would you be interested in receiving information on other marriage support programs, e.g., Worldwide Marriage Encounter? (See *foryourmarriage.org* for a list of marriage support programs.)
- Acquire sufficient copies of the prayer aid, paper, pens and pencils, downloadable handouts, evaluation form, and any optional items. Decide if participants' materials will be passed out as needed or if you will make a set of materials available to participants at a table near the entrance or at each seat. If participants will receive a set of materials, collate packets of the materials.
- Arrive at the site early to coordinate the set-up of the chairs in the general session area. If the materials will be at the participants' seats, distribute one set per chair, including pens or pencils.
- Position the staging table in one of two places:
  - — Near the entrance to the room if it will double as a sign-in/registration table—Lay out name tags and markers for people to fill out as they arrive. If applicable, stack the packets of materials for participants to pick up.
  - — By the facilitator's seat if the facilitator will primarily use it—Place any handouts in stacks on the table in the order in which they will be distributed.
- Set up the newsprint and markers (or blackboard, or whiteboard and markers) at the front of the room or someplace else where everyone can see it.

- Set up the prayer space either in the midst of the general session space, at the front, or to one side. Cover the table, and arrange the table cloth, Bible, candle, and cross or crucifix on it. If additional items are needed for a blessing or ritual, arrange them accordingly.
- As people arrive, greet them, invite them to create a name tag, give them their materials (unless materials are at their seats), and direct them to refreshments, if available.

Welcome and Introduction

- Welcome the participants and give them a verbal tour of the space, including where they might go during the break and where refreshments are.
- Introduce the facilitator. (Or if you are both the host and facilitator, introduce yourself.)
- Invite participants to introduce themselves. Also consider asking them to share their response to one of the following:
  - — How long they have been engaged or married
  - — The first wedding they ever attended or were in
  - — Their favorite reading or song on Catholic marriage
  - — A married or engaged couple they admire
  - — One question that they would like to have answered by the end of the session
- Explain the purpose, schedule, and format of the session. Part I of this *Leader's Guide* has most of the information you need for this.
- Share any ground rules or principles that will guide the group's session.
- Distribute the schedule (and handouts, if needed).
- Divide the participants into their small groups, if needed.
  - — Small groups should be no more than five or six people to give everyone the opportunity to participate equally fully.
  - — Small groups do not have to be couples.
  - — Small groups can also be self-selected. One disadvantage of this method is that people who already know each other tend to cluster together in a self-selected small group.
  - — Choose an arbitrary way to divide participants into small groups—for example,

month or year of birth, what part of the city (or county or country) they are from, or how long they have been married.

Opening Prayer

- Ask the leader(s) of prayer—and musicians, if music is part of the prayer—to come forward.
- Readers may come forward or read from their places, depending upon space.
- Invite everyone to gather around the prayer table. If space is tight, ask everyone to stand.
- When prayer is finished, ask all participants to sit down.

Thematic Session

- If this session is a continuation of a previous session, review the key takeaways from last time, and find out if anyone wants to add other comments to the list.
- Encourage the participants to write down thoughts or comments in their journals as they listen to the readings throughout the session.
- Introduce and present the theme for the session. Highlight passages from the pastoral letter, USCCA, and CCC that relate to this section, especially when comments or questions directly relate to the citations noted in the guide.
- After the presentation, invite the participants to quickly and briefly share words, phrases, or ideas that stuck in their minds during the presentation or reading. Note these on the newsprint (or blackboard or whiteboard).
- For the "Relationship to Lived Experience" section, share the reflection by reading it aloud, letting participants read it silently from their handouts, or showing a PowerPoint presentation of the story. Ask the participants to share their thoughts. If you are using small groups, give them a set amount of time for this sharing. When time has run out, quiet the groups, and ask the group leaders to share one or two responses each.
- Introduce the journaling method that will be used for the session. Invite the participants to begin their journaling. Tell the participants how much time they have for journaling. When time is up, call them back to the next event in the schedule.

- Repeat the above process for each theme.
- Take breaks as scheduled. Make yourself available to the participants during breaks for further discussion. If lunch is scheduled, allow adequate time for serving and eating the meal. The sample session schedules allot about thirty to forty-five minutes for this.

Closing and Key Takeaways

- Wrap up the discussion.
- Ask the participants to respond to the following questions:
  — What key ideas, insights, or learnings did you expect to take away from this session?
  — What key ideas, insights, or learnings are you taking away from this session?.
- Note answers to both questions on the newsprint (or blackboard or whiteboard). Compare the two lists. What are the differences? What are the similarities? Invite anyone to comment on what they see in the comparison between the two.
- If additional sessions are planned, note any pre-session reading that participants could do. Provide them with the Web address(es) of those materials that are located online.
- Remind them of their next steps in journaling.
- Thank the host and any other leaders who helped with the session.
- If this was part of a multi-evening event or a multi-day retreat, remind everyone of the date and starting time for the next session. If possible, encourage all to read the material for the next session(s) online.

Evaluation
(only at the end of the final session)

- Distribute the written evaluation forms. Give participants five minutes to complete the forms.
- Ask for any verbal feedback that may or may not be covered in the evaluation forms. Takes notes on those responses. Include the feedback in your evaluation sent to the pastor, parish committee, or sponsoring organization.
- Following the session, review the written evaluations and compile a summary of the participants' responses for the sponsoring organization.

- Write an evaluation of the session(s) from your perspective. At the beginning, note your recommendations for any future session(s), especially any adjustments to the schedule or setting, any changes to the content, and any issues, concerns, or needs raised by participants that need to be followed up immediately or individually.
- Deliver the summary as requested by the sponsor.

Closing Prayer

- Ask the leader(s) of prayer—and musicians, if music is part of the prayer—to come forward.
- Readers may come forward or read from their places, depending upon space.
- Invite everyone to gather around the prayer table. If space is tight, ask everyone to stand.
- When prayer is finished, invite participants to continue their conversations and enjoy the refreshments, if time allows.

D. Sample Session Schedules

Discussion and reflection on the seven themes may be held in single or multiple sessions. The following are suggested schedules for single-evening and multiple-evening sessions and for one-day and two-day weekend retreats.

Schedule for Single Evening
(Total time: 2 to 2½ hours)

- Welcome and introduction (5-10 minutes)
- Opening prayer (5-15 minutes)
- Part I: Themes 1-3 (15 minutes each)
- Break (5-10 minutes)
- Part II: Themes 4-7 (15 minutes each)
- Closing discussion, evaluation, and prayer (5-15 minutes)

Schedules for Multiple Evenings

Seven Sessions
(Total time: 90 minutes each; one theme per session)

- Welcome and introduction (5-10 minutes)
- Opening prayer (5-15 minutes)
- Present the theme for the session (5-10 minutes)
- Share related references from the pastoral letter, the *United States Catholic Catechism for Adults*, and the *Catechism of the Catholic Church* (5-10 minutes)
- Read and discuss the "Reflection" from "Relationship to Lived Experience" (10-15 minutes)
- Break (5-10 minutes)
- Discussion and journaling (15-20 minutes)
- Closing and key takeaways (5 minutes)
- Evaluation (5 minutes)—Last session only
- Prayer (5 minutes)

Four Sessions
(Total time: 90 minutes each; two themes per session except fourth session)

Sessions 1-3

- Welcome and introduction (5-10 minutes)
- Opening prayer (5-15 minutes)
- Part I: First theme for the session (20-25 minutes each)
- Break (5-10 minutes)
- Part II: Second theme for the session (20-25 minutes each)
- Closing and key takeaways (5 minutes)
- Prayer (5 minutes)

Session 4

- Welcome (5 minutes)
- Opening prayer (5-15 minutes)
- Part I: Last theme (20-25 minutes each)
- Break (5-10 minutes)
- Closing and key takeaways (15-20 minutes)
- Evaluation (10-15 minutes)
- Prayer (5-10 minutes)

Two Sessions
(Total time: 2 to 2½ hours each)

Session 1

- Welcome and introduction (5-10 minutes)
- Opening prayer (5-15 minutes)
- Part I: Themes 1-2 (20-25 minutes each)
- Break (5-10 minutes)
- Part II: Themes 3-4 (20-25 minutes each)
- Closing and key takeaways (5 minutes)
- Prayer (5 minutes)

Session 2

- Welcome (5 minutes)
- Opening prayer (5-15 minutes)
- Part I: Themes 5-6 (20-25 minutes each)
- Break (5-10 minutes)
- Part II: Theme 7 (20-25 minutes)
- Closing, key takeaways, and evaluation (15-20 minutes)
- Prayer (5-10 minutes)

Schedules for Weekend Retreats

One-Day Format
(Total time: 6 to 7 hours)

- Welcome and introduction (10-20 minutes)
- Opening prayer (10-15 minutes)
- Part I: Themes 1-2 (35-40 minutes each)
- Break (10-15 minutes)
- Part II: Themes 3-4 (35-40 minutes each)
- Lunch (30-45 minutes)
- Part III: Themes 5-6 (35-40 minutes each)
- Break (10-15 minutes)
- Part IV: Theme 7 (35-40 minutes)
- Closing and key takeaways (15-20 minutes)
- Evaluation (15-20 minutes)
- Closing prayer (5-10 minutes)

Two-Day Format
(Total time: 1½ days; or 7 to 10½ hours)

Day 1 (Total time: 2 to 3 hours)

- Welcome and introduction (10-20 minutes)
- Opening prayer (15-20 minutes)
- Part I: Theme 1 (40-45 minutes)
- Break (10-15 minutes)
- Part II: Theme 2 (40-45 minutes)
- Evening prayer (10-20 minutes)

Day 2 (Total time: 5 to 7½ hours)

- Morning prayer (10-20 minutes)
- Part III: Theme 3 (40-45 minutes each)
- Break (10-15 minutes)
- Part IV: Theme 4 (40-45 minutes each)
- Break (10-15 minutes)
- Part V: Theme 5 (40-45 minutes each)
- Lunch (30-45 minutes)
- Part VI: Theme 6 (40-45 minutes each)
- Break (10-15 minutes)
- Part VII: Theme 7 (40-45 minutes)
- Closing and key takeaways (20-25 minutes)
- Evaluation (15-20 minutes)
- Closing prayer (10-20 minutes)

PART II

THE SEVEN THEMES

THEME 1: A NATURAL AND SUPERNATURAL GIFT

From the Pastoral Letter *Marriage: Love and Life in the Divine Plan*
This theme is addressed in the following sections of the pastoral letter:
Part I: What Is Marriage?
Part II: Marriage Restored in Christ
Part II: Christian Marriage as a Sacrament

Background for the Facilitator

When the bishops of the United States wrote *Marriage: Love and Life in the Divine Plan*, they deliberately began by discussing marriage as a natural institution. The bishops reasoned that before we can understand marriage as a sacrament, we need to understand marriage as a natural blessing that comes to us from God the Creator.

As humankind's oldest institution, marriage cuts across time and cultures. It has been understood differently in different societies. Today, Western society regards marriage primarily as an interpersonal relationship built on love. This is a relatively new development in human history. Not too long ago, most marriages were arranged based on economic, political, or other utilitarian reasons—usually not love. The Church's understanding of the supernatural gift of marriage that draws on Scripture and Tradition has been held for some two thousand years and has also included the notion of an interpersonal relationship built on love.

Although marriage has looked different throughout the ages, it nevertheless retains its God-given permanent characteristics. It is the permanent, faithful union between a man and a woman, intended for the good of the spouses and for the bearing and raising of children. Both of these purposes contribute to the good of society.

Marriage is a natural gift to society; it is also a supernatural gift to the Church. Christ himself raised it to the dignity of a sacrament. Sacramental marriage does not replace natural marriage but, in a marvelous example of grace building on nature, raises it so that the spouses share in God's own divine life.

Because marriage is God's gift, the Church is committed to supporting all marriages. It should be stressed that if only one spouse or neither spouse is a baptized Christian (e.g., two Jews, or a Catholic and a Muslim), the marriage is a good and natural marriage, albeit nonsacramental. In either case, the Church's law recognizes the marriage. That is why any question of invalidity or dissolution must be taken to a church court, or tribunal.

Breaking Open the Theme with the Group

Our Christian faith tells us that all of life is a gift. The pastoral letter invites us to examine one of God's most fundamental gifts: marriage, which is a both natural and supernatural reality. The natural institution of marriage is a gift in the order of creation. The Sacrament of Matrimony is a gift in the order of the new creation.

Sacred Scripture reveals that God designed marriage for the well-being of his people. Marriage is a natural blessing or gift that affects everyone because it nurtures spouses, creates family, and builds up society. It is true to say that the future of humanity depends on marriage and the family.

Marriage has God as its author. He established it from the beginning of creation with its own structure and proper laws (*Catechism of the Catholic Church*, no. 1603).[1] In the contemporary world, where the spotlight is often on the talents and abilities of men and women, it is easy to think that marriage is a human invention. Our faith tells us otherwise: "Marriage is not . . . the effect of chance or the product of evolution of unconscious natural forces, it is the wise institution of the Creator to realize in mankind His design of love" (Pope Paul VI, *Humanae Vitae*, no. 8).

Marriage is a blessing that God gave men and women for the good of humanity. So essential is this blessing that it was not lost by original sin. Rather it was redeemed by Christ and elevated by him to become one of the seven sacraments for those who are baptized. In this way, Christ restored the original blessing of marriage to its fullness by making it a sign or visible embodiment of his love for the Church. Marriage in the Lord means that authentic human married love "is caught up into divine love and is directed and enriched by the redemptive power of Christ and the salvific action of the Church, with the result that the spouses are effectively led to God and are helped and strengthened in their lofty role as fathers and mothers" (Second Vatican Council, *Pastoral Constitution on the Church in the Modern World* [*Gaudium et Spes*], no. 48).[2]

Because it is fundamentally a gift, marriage is something we are to receive with gratitude and to live out according to God's plan. It is also a gift that the spouses make to one another when they give themselves freely and accept the other completely. Finally, their marriage can be a gift that the couple makes to the community when their love overflows to bear and nurture children, when they serve the needs of others, and when they give witness to God's mercy and love in all aspects of their life.

Foundational Reading

United States Catholic Catechism for Adults

Chapter 21. The Sacrament of Marriage
    The section "God Is the Author of Marriage" further elaborates on the *Catechism's* discussion of marriage in the order of creation.

Catechism of the Catholic Church

CCC, nos. 1601-1605
    These paragraphs from Article 7, "The Sacrament of Matrimony," look at matrimonial covenant as a reflection of the place of marriage in God's plan, especially in the order of creation.

Relationship to Lived Experience

Reflection

Many neighborhoods are blessed to have a married couple on the block who are the true community makers. This is the couple on whom everyone counts to generate enthusiasm for the block party or to make the first welcoming visit to new arrivals. When this special couple also happens to be Christian, their positive influence gives the Church a good name. People seek their opinion on moral questions or ask them to pray for their loved ones. They seem to enjoy working together in the yard and on church projects. Their dinner table always has room for another teenager. In such a couple, people witness the natural and supernatural dimensions of marriage in the flesh.

Discussion Questions

1. Think of a couple whose marriage you admire. Why do you admire them? What would you say are their best qualities?
2. What seems to make a marriage strong, despite the flaws of the spouses?
3. In what ways can your marriage become a gift to other people, not only to each other?
4. What practical steps could you take to extend encouragement or support to another couple who are struggling?
5. What signs do you see that the love of a husband and wife benefits society?

Journaling Questions

1. How has your spouse been a gift to you?
2. What would you like to do for your spouse that would express your love in a special way? Write down a plan for doing it, and follow your plan.

3. A couple who need our encouragement and prayers are _____. What can we do for them, individually or together? (Some suggestions: Babysit for their children while the couple goes on a date; write them a note of encouragement; invite them to work with us on a project in the parish or neighborhood.)

Notes

1 *Catechism of the Catholic Church* (2nd ed.) (Washington, DC: Libreria Editrice Vaticana–United States Conference of Catholic Bishops, 2000). All quotations from the *Catechism of the Catholic Church* in this resource refer to this edition.

2 All quotations from the Second Vatican Council in this resource are taken from Austin Flannery (ed.), *Vatican Council II: Volume 1: The Conciliar and Post Conciliar Documents* (Northport, NY: Costello Publishing, 1996).

THEME 2: UNIQUE UNION OF A MAN AND A WOMAN

From the Pastoral Letter *Marriage: Love and Life in the Divine Plan*
This theme is addressed in the following sections of the pastoral letter:
Part I: Male-Female Complementarity Is Essential to Marriage
Part I: Fundamental Challenges to the Nature and Purposes of Marriage

Background for the Facilitator

Not too long ago, few people questioned that, by definition, marriage is between one man and one woman. In recent years, however, a growing movement has worked to make same-sex unions the legal equivalent of marriage. Proponents argue that the ability to marry anyone of their choosing is a civil right. Denial of this "right," they say, amounts to unjust discrimination. In some states, these efforts have succeeded.

The Church regards same-sex unions as a grave threat because they challenge the very meaning and purpose of marriage. As we saw in Theme 1, God himself is the author of marriage, and he endowed it with certain characteristics. Marriage is between a man and a woman. Human beings are not free to change or redefine this essential characteristic of marriage.

The USCCB statement *Between Man and Woman* explains why marriage can only be between one man and one woman. It also makes these important points:

- Marriage is more than a relationship between a man and a woman. It is the foundation of the family, which is the basic unit of society. Marriage is a personal relationship with public significance.
- Marriage is the basic pattern for male-female relationships. It models how men and women live interdependently, committed to seeking each other's good.

- Marriage provides the best conditions for raising children: the stable, loving relationship of a mother and father.
- It is not unfair to deny legal status to same-sex unions because marriage and same-sex unions are essentially different realities. To treat different things differently is not unjust discrimination.

Breaking Open the Theme with the Group

In the beginning, says Sacred Scripture, God created man and woman in his image, "male and female he created them" (Gn 1:27). With this act, God completes creation and judges it to be "very good" (Gn 1:31). The creation stories communicate essential truths about the fundamental equality and dignity of man and woman as persons and about the fact that both sexes are necessary in God's plan.

The pastoral letter *Marriage: Love and Life in the Divine Plan* points out that the division of humanity into male and female is willed by God. This teaching conveys the truth that male-female complementarity based on sexual difference is essential to the nature and purposes of marriage. Simply put, only a man and a woman can form the intimate union of love and life that is properly called marriage.

In his wisdom, God planned that man and woman would be made for each other. God willed that man and woman would hold something different and distinct in their sexes that, when brought together in union, would uniquely complement each other. The cry of Adam upon seeing Eve that this one "at last, is bone of my bones and flesh of my flesh" (Gn 2:23) is an ancient confirmation of the truth and goodness of God's design.

The mystery of what it means to be human includes the sexual differences that exist between men and women. These differences are willed and blessed by God. They can be seen not only in biological terms but also in how we think, express ourselves, and even pray. A most obvious difference can be seen in the separate gifts a man and a woman bring to sexual intercourse. Together, they jointly hold the potential to bring new life into the world.

The unique complementarity between the man and the woman reaches its fullness in marriage because it is in marriage that the "communion of persons" is formed. As the pastoral letter notes, forming a communion of persons is everyone's vocation because it signifies a call to love like God loves—to thoroughly give one's self to others. The marital communion is unique because it expresses a special type of living for others. Marriage brings together the full gifts of the male and the female with their potential to bring new life into the world, thereby forming the family.

Foundational Reading

United States Catholic Catechism for Adults

Chapter 21. The Sacrament of Marriage
Three sections—"God Is the Author of Marriage," "Christ's Teaching on Marriage," and "The Purposes of Marriage"—go into greater depth on the unique union of man and woman.

Catechism of the Catholic Church

CCC, nos. 1643-1645, 1646-1651
These paragraphs discuss the Church's teaching on conjugal love, the unity and indissolubility of marriage, and marital fidelity.

Relationship to Lived Experience

Reflection

She proudly thinks of herself as a multi-tasker, able to juggle many things at once. Her husband might counter that he likes to concentrate on one thing at a time, focusing his attention on the task at hand. She may need to share her worries; he may be surprised to find that she isn't expecting him to fix them. He discovers that she needs to talk and relax into feeling romantic; she wishes he figured that out sooner. The beauty of marriage is that spouses have a lifetime to understand and appreciate their differences. *Vive la difference!*

Discussion Questions

1. How have society's images of masculinity and femininity changed since your parents' day? How are they the same?
2. Name three ways in which your spouse's approach to problems differs from how you like to do things.
3. Men: What unique qualities do you bring to relationships, both at work and in your family? Women: What unique qualities do you bring to relationships, both at work and in your family?
4. What do you enjoy about being a woman or a man?

Journaling Questions

1. In his wisdom, God planned that man and woman would be made for each other. How would you say that your spouse has been made for you?
2. How does being a man or woman affect how you approach your relationship with God?
3. In our sexual relationship, one thing my spouse could do for me is _____.
   Choose a quiet moment to share this with your spouse.

THEME 3: COMMUNION OF LOVE AND LIFE

From the Pastoral Letter *Marriage: Love and Life in the Divine Plan*
This theme is addressed in the following sections of the pastoral letter:
Part I: The Two Ends or Purposes of Marriage
Part I: How Are the Two Ends of Marriage Related?
Part I: Fundamental Challenges to the Nature and Purposes of Marriage
Part II: Marriage as a Reflection of the Life of the Trinity

Background for the Facilitator

Before the Second Vatican Council, the Church understood marriage in terms of its primary end (the procreation and education of children) and secondary end (the good of the spouses, also called the unitive meaning of marriage). In 1930, with Pope Pius XI's encyclical *Casti Connubii*, the Church began to deepen its understanding of the purposes of marriage. This movement culminated in the Second Vatican Council's affirmation of marriage in more personal categories: as an "intimate partnership of life and . . . love" (*Gaudium et Spes*, no. 48).

Today the Church stresses that the two ends of marriage are equal and inseparable and that they make up the nature of marriage. This teaching is especially important in contemporary society, which has experienced a growing disconnect between marriage and children.

One trend is that some couples deliberately choose to remain childless. They may see children as burdensome, a perception that is prevalent within society. They may place careers above children. They may overemphasize the good of their spousal companionship, not understanding the call to share their love with children.

As part of the National Pastoral Initiative for Marriage, the Catholic bishops of the United States explored this issue with a cross-section of canon (church) lawyers. The canonists, who handle annulment cases in their dioceses, observed that for some couples the idea of children as part of marriage is an afterthought. Engaged couples often do not talk about children—how many they want, when to have them, how to raise them. Rarely do couples say from the beginning that they will *not* have children. Rather, this is a decision that happens gradually, over time. But it is a decision that is increasingly seen as distinct from the decision to get married and to remain married.

On the other hand, with the social stigma largely removed, more single persons are deciding to have their own biological children or to adopt. In 2007, nearly four in ten births were to unmarried women, many of them in cohabiting relationships (National Center for Health Statistics). Unfortunately, children in single-parent households are at risk for unfavorable outcomes. They are more likely to be poor and to abuse alcohol and drugs, and they are less likely to attend college. When they marry, they have an increased chance of divorce.

Wisely, then, the Church holds up the two ends of marriage as intimately tied to each other. In accord with the divine plan, husband and wife generously welcome the gift of children, and their stable, loving relationship provides the environment in which children flourish.

Breaking Open the Theme with the Group

Sacred Scripture reveals that God is love (1 Jn 4:8), that the world was created out of his love (Gn 1:1-26), and that men and women were created in God's image (Gn 1:27). The Church understands that people are therefore made to love like God. Since God is a communion of three loving persons, to be made in God's image means that men and women are called to form relationships that are a communion of persons. This is why the Church teaches that God has given all his children a vocation to love like him. It is a universal call to holiness. These foundational teachings take on a special meaning in marriage.

Marriage is a unique communion of persons because God designed it to bring together the totality of a man and a woman—body, mind, and soul—to love and give life. Marriage creates a "one-flesh" union (Gn 2:24; Mt 19:6ff.). In creating man and woman for each other, God made marriage to be love-giving and life-giving. We call these two purposes or ends of marriage the *unitive* and the *procreative*. They are inseparably connected and are ordered to each other. The two purposes cannot be separated "without altering the couple's spiritual life and compromising the goods of marriage and the future of the family" (*Catechism of the Catholic Church*, no. 2363).

When a man and a woman exchange marital consent, they establish a partnership for the whole of life. They mutually vow an exclusive fidelity that is open to the procreation and nurturing of children. In participating in God's love, husband and wife are empowered to make a total gift of self to each other. As spouses, husband and wife exist not only side by side with each other but also mutually for each other.

A husband and wife serve as a symbol of both life and love in a way that no other relationship of human persons can. As the pastoral letter *Marriage: Love and Life in the Divine Plan* says, if procreation is a true participation in the creative activity of God, then it is a work that is inseparable from self-gift.

As stewards of the gifts of love and life, spouses hold the responsibility to nurture marital love and its life-giving potential. Sexual intercourse is the act that signifies and embodies the marital covenant. This is why the Church teaches that each act of sexual intercourse must be open to life, because the whole meaning of marriage is present and signified in each marital act.

The pastoral letter points out that contraception is "objectively wrong" because it deliberately separates the unitive purpose from the procreative purpose of marriage. It also notes why natural methods of family planning are different from contraception. Natural methods are not good merely because they are natural. Rather, they are good because they respect God's design for married love.

Foundational Reading

United States Catholic Catechism for Adults

Chapter 21. The Sacrament of Marriage
Chapter 30. The Sixth Commandment: Marital Fidelity

These two chapters develop the unitive purpose of marriage and marital fidelity more deeply, especially two sections of Chapter 21 entitled "The Purposes of Marriage" and "Effects of the Sacrament."

Catechism of the Catholic Church

CCC, nos. 1621-1624, 1643-1654

These paragraphs focus on the celebration of the Sacrament of Marriage, on conjugal love, and on openness to fertility.

Relationship to Lived Experience

Reflection

When they were newlyweds, both were sure that this was the one person who completed their world. They thought they could never love each other more. When they found they could not have biological children, they adopted their little girl and discovered a new dimension to their love. The day they first held her in their arms, they suddenly saw each other in a new light: Mom and Dad. In becoming parents, they began to understand something new about why God had brought them together. Their feelings of great joy were accompanied by feelings of overwhelming responsibility; they knew they would need God's help.

Discussion Questions

1. What can couples who have no difficulty conceiving learn from an adopting couple like the one in the story? In what additional ways can a married couple have a procreative relationship and attitude?
2. Think of a couple with children whose family life you admire. From your observation, how are the children a blessing to that couple's marriage?
3. How can a couple maintain intimacy when they are parents?
4. How can we as a parish communicate the message that children are an important part of marriage?

Journaling Questions

1. In what ways do you and your spouse need to change or grow in order to be able to welcome a child (or another child) into the family?
2. If you are a parent, how has your child been a blessing to you? How have you changed for the better since becoming a parent?
3. If you do not have children, how do you expect that having a child would change your marriage?

THEME 4: SACRAMENT OF CHRIST'S LOVE

From the Pastoral Letter *Marriage: Love and Life in the Divine Plan*
This theme is addressed in the following sections of the pastoral letter:
Part II: Christian Marriage as a Sacrament
Part II: Marriage as a Vocation

Background for the Facilitator

Recent research has yielded valuable insight into Catholics' understanding of the sacraments in general and marriage in particular. Clearly, sacraments play an important role in the spiritual lives of adult Catholics, especially those who are regular Mass-goers. According to a survey by the Center for Applied Research in the Apostolate (CARA), 60 percent of adult Catholics agree that sacraments are essential to their faith, and 89 percent say that marriage is either "somewhat" or "very" meaningful to them.[1]

Seven in ten survey respondents were familiar with the church teaching that marriage between two baptized persons is a sacrament. In general, respondents expressed an understanding of the nature and purposes of marriage that includes beliefs about permanence, commitment, openness to children, the value of spousal love, and the centrality of God in a marriage.

Commenting on the CARA research, the members of the USCCB Subcommittee on Marriage and Family found much that was positive, but they did identify two concerns. First, they noted that 30 percent of Catholics have neither married in the Church nor had their marriage subsequently sanctified by the Church. Second, they remarked upon a growing rate (41 percent) of marriage outside the Church among younger Catholics; moreover, more than half of unmarried young Catholic adults do not consider it important to be married in the Church. According to the subcommittee, "These data may indicate an increasing number of Catholics who are unlikely to experience the full value and graces of the sacrament in the future."

There is ample evidence that couples' understanding of the sacramentality of their union can grow and deepen throughout their marital journey. This was an important finding from diocese-sponsored focus groups held in 2005 and 2006 as part of the National Pastoral Initiative for Marriage. Many longer-married couples described how Christ has sustained their union, especially in difficult times, and helped them to love their spouse in a way that truly images Christ's permanent and unconditional love for the Church.

Breaking Open the Theme with the Group

When we were baptized we were transformed, by the power of the Holy Spirit, into a new creation. We became members of the Body of Christ and were enabled to share in his own divine life. Being a member of the living Body of Christ has profound implications for marriage.

Jesus heals marriage and restores it to its original purity of permanent self-giving in one flesh. But the Lord does not stop there. Christ generously invites husband and wife to participate in his spousal love for his Church. His spousal love is a love "to the end" (Jn 13:1). Jesus thereby sets the standard for marital love. It is a love that is to be total, faithful, permanent, life-giving, and self-giving. Christian spouses are invited to participate in his self-giving love and to model their love on God's inner life and love in the Blessed Trinity. In this way, the marriage of two Christians becomes a living symbol: a sign that makes present the union of Christ with his Church (see Eph 5:22ff.).

The Sacrament of Matrimony does not replace the natural institution of marriage. Rather, it renews the natural institution and elevates it so that it shares in a love larger than itself. Christian marriage, then, is nothing less than a participation in the covenant between Christ and his Church.

The Sacrament of Matrimony, along with the Sacrament of Holy Orders, is called by the *Catechism of the Catholic Church* a "sacrament at the service of communion." This means that the sacrament is directed toward the service of others and that carrying out this service contributes to one's personal salvation. These two sacraments, each in their own way, "confer a particular mission in the Church and serve to build up the People of God" (*Catechism of the Catholic Church*, no. 1534).

Jesus is truly present in his followers and in their marriages. Practically, this means that when life's difficulties press in on husband and wife, they are not alone. Though they remain fallible and weak human beings, Christian spouses can rely on Jesus to help them to continue in love even when it seems impossible. This is what is meant by the grace of the sacrament. In every moment of their married lives, Jesus is present to give Christian spouses the strength to rise again after they have fallen, to forgive one another, to bear one another's burdens . . . to love one another even to the end.

Foundational Reading

United States Catholic Catechism for Adults

Chapter 21. The Sacrament of Marriage
Chapter 28. The Fourth Commandment: Strengthen Your Family
These two chapters discuss "Christ's Teaching on Marriage" and pastoral care for the support of marriage (in the "Do All You Can to Strengthen Your Marriage" and "Divorce and Pastoral Care" sections), including support for families.

Catechism of the Catholic Church

CCC, nos. 1612-1617
These paragraphs elaborate on marriage in the Lord, highlighting the nuptial covenant and explaining Jesus' spousal relationship with the Church as a symbol for marriage.

Relationship to Lived Experience

Reflection

She felt that the world was crashing around her when she learned of her husband's affair. Still, she was determined to fight for her marriage, and he wanted desperately to heal what he had damaged. Popular wisdom was not on their side, and people let her know it, too. After tears and late-night talks, some angry exchanges, and lots of counseling and prayer, she and her husband reconciled. She would say it was faith that made the difference, but mostly they don't explain their decision to others. They just say, "We're married." That was ten years ago, and new friends would never guess what they went through. Most couples will not be so severely tested, but a failure to be forgiving can make even small faults—leaving the cap off the toothpaste, poor hygiene, or weak cooking skills—destructive to a marriage.

Discussion Questions

1. During the course of their marriage, many couples will experience at least one major challenge that threatens to break up the marriage. Besides infidelity, examples include an addiction to drugs, alcohol, or pornography; domestic abuse; and serious financial mismanagement. How could a Christian respond when a friend or family member is experiencing difficulty in marriage? How have you responded in such a situation?
2. What are some of the joyful things about being married? What are some of the challenges? Can something be both joyful and challenging?
3. How can the grace of the Sacrament of Marriage sustain couples in difficult times?
4. How did you learn about the importance of being married in the Church? How could religious

education of children and youth about Christian marriage be improved?

Journaling Questions

1. One way that I could be more giving toward my spouse is _____. Here's how I will do it . . .
2. A difficulty I am dealing with now in my marriage is _____. With whom will I talk about this?

3. How has the grace of the Sacrament of Marriage sustained you in difficult times?
4. Read one of the articles on "For Every Marriage" or the "Marriage Rx" at *www.foryourmarriage.org*. What new ideas did you gain for your marriage?

Note

1 Center for Applied Research in the Apostolate (CARA), *Marriage in the Church: A Survey of U.S. Catholics* (Washington, DC: Georgetown University, 2007).

THEME 5: FOUNDATION OF THE FAMILY AND SOCIETY

From the Pastoral Letter Marriage: Love and Life in the Divine Plan
This theme is addressed in the following sections of the pastoral letter:
Part I: Fundamental Challenges to the Nature and Purposes of Marriage
Part II: The Family as Domestic Church

Background for the Facilitator

Mention the word "church," and most people probably think of their local parish. Some might think of St. Peter's in Rome as symbolic of the worldwide Church. Few, however, would imagine their own family as "church."

The early Church understood the Christian family as an *ecclesia domestica*, or domestic church. This expression dropped out of common usage, only to be recovered during the debates in the Second Vatican Council (1962-1965). The Council realized that the most basic expression of the Church was not the parish but the Christian family. The family, our first community, is the foundational way God gathers us and forms us. Christian families do not simply draw sustenance from the Church; their daily life is a true expression of the Church. They manifest Christ's presence to the world and share in the same mission that Christ gave to the entire Church.

The domestic church rests on the foundation of a baptized husband and wife. They establish a communion of love into which children are welcomed.

The Church has always taught that children do best when raised by two married parents. Social science research confirms this wisdom. Children raised in intact families are generally healthier, less likely to live in poverty, and more likely to attend college. They are less likely to be physically or sexually abused and less likely to use drugs or alcohol. They have a decreased risk of divorcing when they get married. See "Why Marriage Matters: 26 Conclusions from the Social Sciences" at *www. americanvalues.org/html/r-wmm.html*.

These advantages are important, but the Christian couple offer even more to their children. By words and example, they pass on essential teachings on catechesis, prayer, morality, and Christian service. They are models of Christian service, making Christ's presence known by welcoming the stranger and feeding the hungry.

No family does this perfectly; however, as the USCCB statement *Follow the Way of Love* points out, "A family is holy not because it is perfect but because God's grace is at work in it" (9).

Breaking Open the Theme with the Group

In a variety of ways, husband and wife are co-builders of the foundation of all human society. Their union brings families together and begins a new family.

By its nature, marital love is self-giving. It overflows from the spouses to their children, extended family, neighbors, and the wider community. Marital love is literally life-giving. The individual gifts of male and female human fertility are brought together in marriage. When these gifts are joined, the spouses' potential to create new life with God is sacredly entrusted to their care.

Husband and wife are called to a noble task to share their love quite literally with their own children. In opening their hearts to each other and to the Lord of all creation, spouses cooperate with God to build the family. So unique and precious is the gift of life to married couples that the Church can teach that "children are the supreme gift of marriage" (*Gaudium et Spes*, no. 50). The pastoral letter *Marriage: Love and Life in the Divine Plan* explains that children bring joy even in the midst of heartaches; they give added direction to the lives of their parents.

As good stewards, husband and wife are called to nurture and educate their children. The Church teaches that this unique spousal responsibility is integral to being stewards of the gift of life. In fact, through the ages the Church has consistently taught that spouses are called to procreation and to education of their children. They are "fortified and, as it were, consecrated for the duties and dignity of their state" by the Sacrament of Matrimony (*Gaudium et Spes*, no. 48). Husband and wife live a union whose nature is service to others.

By creating a home where love, care, and growth in the faith flourish among family members, married couples reflect the life of the Church in the world. In the family, parents teach their children how to pray, how to embrace God's loving commandments, how to grow in virtue and holiness. The Christian family that celebrates the sacraments, especially the Eucharist, establishes a reciprocal relationship between the family and the entire body of Christ that is the Church.

With so exalted a calling, the Christian family is also a sign and image of the communion of the Father and the Son in the Holy Spirit. The love that spouses have for each other, and that they in turn give their children, overflows from the family members to nurture the world. This familial love supplies an irreplaceable service to society. The Christian family participates in building up the Kingdom of God.

Foundational Reading

United States Catholic Catechism for Adults

Chapter 21. The Sacrament of Marriage
Chapter 28. The Fourth Commandment:
    Strengthen Your Family
These two chapters further explain the relationship between the sacrament and society, especially in these sections: "Effects of the Sacrament," "Do All You Can to Strengthen Marriage," and "Mixed and Interfaith Marriages."

Catechism of the Catholic Church

CCC, nos. 1635-1658, 1666
These paragraphs address mixed marriages, the marriage bond, the grace of the sacrament, conjugal love, and the domestic church.

Relationship to Lived Experience

Reflection

Whenever he heard an ambulance siren, he offered a prayer for those involved in the accident or medical emergency. When the family pet passed away, she took care to bury it lovingly in the garden. Their Catholic faith was evident in the artwork on the walls and in the simple prayers offered at table and at bedtime. They celebrated the anniversary of each child's Baptism with ice cream sundaes, and they always managed to pull together a group of neighbors for Christmas caroling. Their children saw and treasured these rituals of family life.

Discussion Questions

1. Tell about a tradition or ritual you have in your home that you and your children enjoy celebrating each year, perhaps on a holiday or special occasion. Why does your family love doing this?
2. What does your family do that brings you together?
3. What opportunities for passing on your faith are uniquely present in family life (opportunities that don't usually happen at church)?
4. What things or actions remind you of God's presence in your home and family?

Journaling Questions

1. List three lessons you have learned from being a parent. How has parenthood strengthened your faith?
2. What would you like to do differently as a family? What one step can you take right now?
3. In your home, identify some reminders of God's presence. What can you add to or change about your home to increase your awareness of God in your daily life?

THEME 6: JOURNEY OF HUMAN AND SPIRITUAL GROWTH

From the Pastoral Letter *Marriage: Love and Life in the Divine Plan*
This theme is addressed in the following sections of the pastoral letter:
Part II: Growth in Christian Marriage
Part II: Growth in the Virtues

Background for the Facilitator

As discussed in Theme 1, an understanding of marriage as supernatural gift builds on an understanding of marriage as a natural institution. Similarly, spiritual growth in marriage is intertwined with human growth. The spiritual growth of the spouses takes place within the natural growth of the marriage.

Human growth is often discussed in terms of stages. At each stage of life, humans must complete certain developmental tasks before they can move on successfully to the next stage. A person moves towards maturity by integrating the learnings from each stage.

Social scientists have observed that marriages, too, typically move through a series of stages. A healthy, lifelong marriage means building "multiple marriages" with the same spouse. Although the exact number of stages may vary, scientists agree that unique tasks, such as differentiating self from family of origin or forming a marital system, must be mastered to ensure continued healthy development. Movement from one stage to the next, from one level of maturity to a higher level, is always precipitated by transitional events, such as the birth of a child, a job loss, or a major health issue.

Each stage of marriage has its own joys and sorrows, opportunities and challenges. When understood in the light of Christ's own journey, they can contribute to human growth and spiritual maturity. That is, a couple grows in holiness by journeying with Christ through the mystery of his life, death, and Resurrection. This movement through life to death to new life is called the Paschal Mystery. It is the basic model for Christian living and, therefore, for married love.

The Paschal Mystery unfolds again and again through the stages of marriage. There are Holy Thursdays—times of loving service when couples put their own needs in second place. There are Good Fridays—times of suffering, tragedies, even death. There are Holy Saturdays—times of waiting and uncertainty when all seems dark and the couple wonders if their marriage will survive. Then there are Easter Sundays—when the marriage of a child or the birth of a grandchild brings new hope.

These high, low, and ordinary moments of marriage are the raw material from which a life of holiness is fashioned. Holiness is not superimposed upon the couple; it arises from within the marriage. This is why couples often have such a strong sense of becoming holy together, of leading each other to God. The process that leads to a successful marriage can also lead to a holy marriage.

Breaking Open the Theme with the Group

When a man and a woman marry, they embark on a mutual journey of human and spiritual growth. Any married couple can testify that marriage requires persistent effort, that there are times when one seems to be knocked down and must find the strength to get up again. The pastoral letter *Marriage: Love and Life in the Divine Plan* challenges couples not only to persevere but also to aspire to become fully what they are, namely, a living image of Christ's love for the Church. The practice of virtues will enable them to do this.

Practicing virtues enables us to have a mindset that seeks to do the good. The *Catechism* says that virtue "allows the person not only to perform good acts, but to give the best of himself" (*Catechism of the Catholic Church*, no. 1803). The pastoral letter notes that growth in virtue helps husband and wife to acquire the interior qualities that open them to God's love and that allow them to share in his love more deeply. As individuals and couples grow in virtue, they grow in holiness.

The foundational set of virtues that assist husband and wife are the theological virtues of faith, hope, and charity. Faith in Jesus and his Gospel calls Christians to an ever deeper discipleship with all of its richness. Hope provides the confidence that God's love will never abandon them and their family. Charity pervades everything that they are and do because their love mirrors that of Christ.

The principal moral virtues are rooted in the theological virtues. Therefore, the practice of prudence, justice, fortitude, and temperance is especially helpful for human and spiritual growth in marriage. These very practical virtues can lead husband and wife to greater emotional maturity. They can help spouses put their challenges and sorrows into perspective.

Jesus lives in and with husband and wife, ever ready to support and transform their love. This is a lifetime adventure in mutual striving to grow closer to each other in Christ. To live his generous, self-giving love as husband and wife is the vocation of a married couple. Marriage is an authentic vocation within the life of the Church. Like all vocations, it is a specific way of participating in the universal call to holiness and the imitation of God's love. The pastoral letter urges Christian spouses to journey in Christ toward the discovery of an intimacy that is deeply satisfying because it is a participation in the intimate self-giving of Christ.

Foundational Reading

United States Catholic Catechism for Adults

Chapter 21. The Sacrament of Marriage
Chapter 23. Life in Christ—Part One
These two chapters link human and spiritual growth, especially as discussed in the sections titled "Effects of the Sacrament" (Chapter 21) and "The Excellence of Virtues" (Chapter 23).

Catechism of the Catholic Church

CCC, nos. 1803-1804, 1812-1829, 1601-1658, 1655-1659
These paragraphs go into depth on the Church's teaching on the virtues, especially the theological virtues of faith, hope, and love, which are echoed in the sections on the Sacrament of Marriage and the family as the domestic church.

Relationship to Lived Experience

Reflection

When he returned from his tour in Iraq, the baby was nine months old. He felt like an outsider in his own family. There was no way he could fully explain what his past year had been like, and he had missed so much at home. The baby didn't know him and certainly didn't seem to need anyone but Mom. His wife was thrilled that he was home, but she resented that his return had thrown a wrench into her well-established routine. They felt a great distance between them. Memories of the happy days when they were first married helped to give them faith that God meant for them to be together, and they looked with hope to better days ahead. She found support from other military spouses; he found sound advice in his talks with their pastor. Now, their baby is four years old. Their marriage and their family bond are strong. They volunteer as a mentor couple to support other military couples struggling with similar transitions.

Discussion Questions

1. Make a map of the different "marriages" you have experienced. What events were the transition points that caused each change?
2. How has surviving a time of trial, either personally or in your marriage, better equipped you to support others who are suffering or struggling?
3. How can a church community help families in times of transition and loss, e.g., families experiencing a death or birth, empty-nest couples, parents of teens?

Journaling Questions

1. Write a prayer for your spouse, expressing your hopes and dreams for him or her.
2. Think of a time from the past when your marriage went through a transition. Describe life before, during, and after the transition. What got you through? How was God present to you?
3. What have you done for your marriage lately? It doesn't have to be something big. For ideas, take one of the quizzes or view the videos of other couples' responses at *www.foryourmarriage.org*. Write about your responses.

THEME 7: SCHOOL OF LOVE AND GRATITUDE

From the Pastoral Letter *Marriage: Love and Life in the Divine Plan*
This theme is addressed in the following sections of the pastoral letter:
Part II: Growth Toward Perfection
Part II: Marriage and the Eucharist

Background for the Facilitator

A marriage is many things. Good marriages provide companionship, intimacy, mutual support, and friendship ("I married my best friend"). Marriage is a partnership for raising children; it is also an economic and financial partnership.

A Christian marriage is all this and more. In the diocese-sponsored focus groups mentioned in Theme 4, many couples expressed a sense of "leading each other to heaven." They understand that marriage is a distinct call to grow in holiness, a call that is set within the universal call to holiness, as the Second Vatican Council taught (see *Dogmatic Constitution on the Church* [*Lumen Gentium*], no. 11).

Another way to say this is that couples are called to grow in virtue, including those virtues that are especially applicable to marriage. Examples include patience, humility, and chastity. The pastoral letter *Marriage: Love and Life in the Divine Plan* singles out gratitude as a virtue that is frequently overlooked in relation to married life. Often, for example, spouses are more likely to say "thank you" to a stranger than to each other. Spouses who rarely hear an expression of gratitude can feel taken for granted, resentful, angry, or rejected.

The pastoral letter goes so far as to call marriage a "school" for nurturing gratitude for the gift of one's spouse and the other gifts that are proper to married love. A couple who strive to grow in gratitude will, inevitably, grow in other virtues as well. The virtues do not develop separately; they are intertwined. A husband who is grateful for the gift of his wife will humbly put her needs above his own. The grateful wife will endure her husband's all-too-human failings with patience and good humor. Both will practice chastity in order to safeguard the great good of their union. In ways great and small, the couple will grow in virtue and in love, which includes all the virtues.

Breaking Open the Theme with the Group

As Adam recognized Eve as God's gift to him, likewise, spouses should recognize each other as God's gift in their lives. Through life's journey, sometime a husband or wife may need to reflect on the gift of the other, especially when misunderstandings or difficulties arise. To remember how this person came to offer love so unexpectedly or how one recognized the other as "made for me" is to be humbled by divine gift. In those moments of remembering, thankfulness should fill one's heart. Spousal gratitude is linked to conjugal charity. It will help husband and wife to persevere in fidelity, kindness, communication, and mutual assistance.

Gratitude opens the human heart to receive further gifts from God. For those who are married, gratefulness for God's gifts includes openness to the gift of children. It means building a family. Sometimes God may ask spouses to open their homes to foster children, other relatives, or neighbors, or to anyone in need. As the words of the final blessing from the Rite of Marriage pray: "May you always bear witness to the love of God in this world so that the afflicted and needy will find in you generous friends, and welcome you into the joys of heaven."[1]

The pastoral letter on marriage also turns our attention to the relationship between Christian spouses and the Eucharist. The interior posture of gratitude that should permeate husband and wife is poured out in their mutual gratitude to God for Jesus in the Eucharist. It is Christ who dwells with them and sustains them in their sacrament. When Catholic spouses receive Jesus in the Eucharist, they encounter the source from which their own marriage covenant flows and the source from which it is renewed.

Persevering in Christ's love changes the Christian husband and wife. They become a sign of the Kingdom of God. When married couples grow in holiness, they reveal the joy of a life lived in love and gratitude. They become a blessing and gift to each other and to the world. In Christ, husband and wife become what they are, a sign of hope, because the love of Christ moves the married couple to ever greater heights of love.

Foundational Reading

United States Catholic Catechism for Adults

Chapter 23. Life in Christ—Part One
Chapter 28. The Fourth Commandment:
Strengthen Your Family
Chapter 30. The Sixth Commandment:
Marital Fidelity
These chapters explore how a husband and wife demonstrate gratitude to God by living a virtuous and faith-filled marriage.

Catechism of the Catholic Church

CCC, nos. 897- 913, 2023-2014, 2028-2029
The first paragraphs highlight the vocation of lay people and their participation in Christ's prophetic and kingly office. The remaining paragraphs focus on sanctifying grace as the gratuitous gift of God and as that which makes us pleasing to him, and on our response to this grace.

Relationship to Lived Experience

Reflection

Watching her husband reading to their young children one evening, her heart swelled in gratitude for the tender and loving man that God had made for her. Catching her look of love, he paused and looked deeply into her eyes, returning her smile. He savored the moment of peace and the warmth of his family surrounding him, thinking that he certainly had so much to be grateful for. Later, after the children were tucked in bed, she embraced him and told him how grateful she was to have him. He told her, "God has given us so much, I've been feeling lately like we certainly have a lot to offer another child . . ."

Discussion Questions

1. How do spouses show gratitude toward each other? Are some ways more effective than others?
2. How can spouses help each other to share the gift of themselves with others, both inside and outside of their family?

Provide index cards for question 3 and 4.

3. What good thing did your spouse do recently that you could have thanked him or her for, but didn't? Write it down on the index card. Share the card privately with your spouse. (The facilitator can also invite anyone who wishes to share.)
4. Make a list: What do you still love about your spouse? Exchange cards.

Journaling Questions

1. Write your love story, as you want it told to your great-grandchildren. Include how and why you fell for your spouse. Recount at least one way your spouse gave of himself or herself.
2. What gifts has God given you in your spouse and your marriage? With whom will you share them?
3. List five ways that you show gratitude toward your spouse. Which two ways does he or she like best? Resolve to do those two more often.

Note

1 Rite of Marriage A, no. 125, in *The Rites of the Catholic Church* (New York: Pueblo Publishing, 1976).

PART III

_____ ◯◯ _____

SOURCES

Part III includes the "starter list" of Vatican, papal, USCCB, and prayer resources available. Additional recommendations to these lists can be found at *www.usccb.org/loveandlife*. Many of these publications and resources can be ordered in print from the USCCB (*www.usccbpublishing.org*).

A. HIGHLIGHTING MARRIAGE IN THE PARISH

Implement any of the following suggestions to draw attention to the importance of marriage in the life of the parish, to support married couples as they travel through various stages of their marriage, and to educate the parish on the role and significance of marriage in the Catholic faith.

Marriage Education and Enrichment

- Invite a couple who have been married for many years, or a couple who are active in ministry/community service together, to share their experiences at an evening reception or morning brunch. Invite married, engaged, and dating couples to attend.
- Marriage is celebrated with different customs in different cultures. Host a marriage enrichment evening that includes a presentation of wedding and courtship customs from many cultures.
- Celebrate the unique qualities of men and women in your community by offering a men's night or ladies' night at your parish. Invite a speaker who focuses on the special gifts of the opposite sex.
- Sponsor a couples' book club. For book ideas see *www.foryourmarriage.org*.
- Host instruction in natural family planning methods at your parish. For educational resources, visit the natural family planning homepage, *www.usccb.org/prolife/issues/nfp/index.shtml*.
- Identify retreat centers in your area that offer couples' retreats. Advertise them in your bulletin. If none exist, organize a retreat for married couples. Consider using this *Leaders' Guide* as a resource.

Families and Parenting

- Build a team of experienced parents to mentor new parents bringing their children for Baptism. This team could be trained to teach baptismal preparation in the home, rather than in a classroom.
- Facilitate outreach to new parents—e.g., meals, shopping, print resources, prayer support, pastoral visits. Remember to include new dads as well as new moms.
- Host a Christian parenting workshop for families of children who have celebrated First Penance and First Communion.
- Supply family prayer helps and rituals for the home during Advent, Christmas, and Lent; before vacation season; and at the beginning of the school year.
- Invite three couples with children to participate in small family-style faith sharing groups at the parish. Provide childcare for a portion of the meetings, offering the adults time to discuss and socialize.
- At an August Mass, publicly acknowledge college students or young adults who are moving away. Utilize a ritual blessing such as "Blessing Before Leaving Home for School, Employment, Deployment, or Ministry" found in the revised edition of *Catholic Household Blessings and Prayers*.[1] Invite the students and their families to a reception following Mass as an opportunity for networking with other families in similar transition.
- Build more catechesis on Christian marriage into youth ministry programs, fostering the value of celebrating weddings in the Church with the community of faith.

Service

- Arrange an opportunity for married couples to serve on a parish project or event as a couple, giving visible witness to their joint vocation to serve the community.
- Create a team of volunteers who can serve as wedding coordinators, assisting couples in planning their church weddings. These volunteers can help at the rehearsal and attend the wedding as ministers of hospitality. Simplify parish policies about weddings.
- Compile a list of qualified marriage counselors to whom parish staff can refer couples who come seeking help with marital difficulties.
- Create and make available a directory of parish and diocesan support groups for couples in transition: loss of a child, terminal illness, empty-nesters, widows and widowers, blended families, and so forth. Post it on the parish Web site.

Hospitality and Celebration

- Organize a parish welcome ministry to orient new members. Have volunteers call new parishioners and invite them to the monthly welcome and orientation coffee in their home or at the parish center. Provide information and recommendations about area stores, restaurants, service providers, recreation and playgrounds, and so on. Share the "insider's tips" about your town, and ask what the newcomers need. Provide information about opportunities for parish involvement.
- Recognize milestone wedding anniversaries (first, fifth, tenth, twentieth, etc.) in your parish bulletin. Congratulate the couple. Include a wedding picture, if space allows and the couple are comfortable with it.
- Reach out to couples who want to explore convalidating their civil marriages. Provide marriage preparation designed especially for convalidating couples.
- If a seminarian is temporarily assigned to your parish, organize couples to host him for dinner in their home during his stay.

Note

1 USCCB, *Catholic Household Blessings and Prayers*, rev. ed. (Washington, DC: USCCB, 2007), 284.

B. REFERENCE RESOURCES

These titles are organized by level of authority of the author and document, and then by how relevant they are to the topic of marriage.

Vatican/Papal Documents

Catechism of the Catholic Church, 2nd ed. (Washington, DC: Libreria Editrice Vaticana–USCCB, 2000). See key passages on marriage that are cited throughout this *Leader's Guide*.

Second Vatican Council. Selected passages from the *Pastoral Constitution on the Church in the Modern World* (*Gaudium et Spes*) (December 1965), nos. 47-52. Key passages include the dignity of marriage, the role of the family, and the duty of society and the Church to support families. Various translations of Vatican II documents exist; they can also be found in English at the Vatican Web site at *www.vatican.va*.

Pope John Paul II. *On the Family* (*Familiaris Consortio*) (December 15, 1981). Washington, DC: USCCB, 1982. *www.vatican.va*. This foundational document discusses the nature and tasks of the Christian family and the scope of pastoral care needed by families; it describes marriage as a covenant relationship and family as domestic church.

Pope John Paul II. *Letter to Families* (*Gratissimam Sane*) (February 2, 1994). *www.vatican.va*. Writing during the International Year of the Family, Pope John Paul II reflects upon the communion of persons as the foundation of the civilization of love.

Pope John Paul II. *On the Dignity and Vocation of Women* (*Mulieris Dignitatem*) (August 15, 1988), no. 15. *www.vatican.va*. This apostolic letter highlights the nature and dignity of women, the complementarity of men and women in marriage, and Mary's essential role in the Church.

Pope Paul VI. *On the Regulation of Birth* (*Humanae Vitae*) (July 25, 1968). Washington, DC: USCCB, 1968. *www.vatican.va*. This authoritative encyclical of Pope Paul VI reconfirms the Church's teaching on the purposes of married love, the gift of fertility, and responsible parenthood.

USCCB Documents

Marriage: Love and Life in the Divine Plan. Washington, DC: USCCB, 2009. In this pastoral letter, the Catholic bishops of the United States explain the foundation for the Church's teachings and practices about marriage. The statement is included at the end of this *Leader's Guide*; individual copies are also available in English and Spanish from *www.usccbpublishing.org*. Also available online at *www.usccb.org/loveandlife*.

Marriage: Love and Life in the Divine Plan: Abridged Version. Washington, DC: USCCB, 2009. This abridgment in brochure form is available in English and Spanish.

United States Catholic Catechism for Adults. Washington, DC: USCCB, 2006. See key passages on marriage that are cited throughout this *Leader's Guide*.

Matrimony: Sacrament of Enduring Love: A Book of Readings on Marriage. Washington, DC: USCCB, in press. This book is a collection of articles on marriage that were originally featured as part of the celebration of Catechetical Sunday 2010. Below are suggested articles from the collection that go with each theme in this *Leader's Guide*. (Note that some articles are suggested under more than one theme.)

Theme 1. A Natural and Supernatural Gift
  • Flores, Bishop Daniel. "Marriage: Sacrament of Enduring Love."
  • Verbeek, Siobhan M. "The Church's Healing Ministry in Caring for Those Touched by the Trauma of Separation and Divorce."

Theme 2. Unique Union of a Man and a Woman
  • Granados, Jose, DCJM. "Theology of the Body: A Catechesis into the Fullness of Love."
  • Kurtz, Archbishop Joseph E. "Responsibility and Joy: Catechesis and the Promotion and Protection of Marriage."

Theme 3. Communion of Love and Life
  • Boadt, Lawrence, CSP, SSD. "Scriptural Reflections on Marriage and Marital Love as Reflective of the Union of God and Israel and Christ and the Church."
  • Granados, Jose, DCJM. "Theology of the Body: A Catechesis into the Fullness of Love."

Theme 4. Sacrament of Christ's Love
  • Flores, Bishop Daniel. "Marriage: Sacrament of Enduring Love."
  • Lombardi, Dominic. "A Model for Immediate Catechesis for the Sacrament of Marriage."

Theme 5. Foundation of the Family and Society
  • Kurtz, Archbishop Joseph E. "Responsibility and Joy: Catechesis and the Promotion and Protection of Marriage."
  • Weinandy, Thomas, OFM Cap. "The Christian Family and the Evangelization of Children."

Theme 6. Journey of Human and Spiritual Growth
  • Anderson, Carl A. "Building Healthy Marriages in Difficult Economic Times."
  • Broglio, Archbishop Timothy P. "Married Couples and the Challenge of Extended Tours, Financial Pressures, and Reentry into the Family After Military Service."
  • Grabowski, John. "Formation in Human Sexuality, Marriage, and Family Life."
  • Meier, Sam, and Beth Meier. "Pornography's Effects on Marriage and the Hope of Recovery and Healing."

Theme 7. School of Love and Gratitude
  • Hater, Robert. "Advent-Christmas and Lenten-Easter Reflections: Cultivating the Gift of Self."
  • Herzog, Bishop Ronald P. "Celebrating the Rite of Marriage."

Follow the Way of Love: A Pastoral Message to Families. Washington, DC: USCCB, 1994. This statement affirms the fundamental dignity of the family and offers a compelling description of the domestic church. Available in English and Spanish.

Between Man and Woman: Questions and Answers About Marriage and Same-Sex Unions. Washington, DC: USCCB, 2003. This brochure presents a cogent summary of church teaching on marriage between a man and woman based on Scripture and Tradition. Available in English and Spanish.

Married Love and the Gift of Life. Washington, DC: USCCB, 2006. This booklet responds to questions about married love and contraception and provides a solid review of natural family planning for engaged and married couples. Available in English and Spanish.

Life-Giving Love in an Age of Technology. Washington, DC: USCCB, 2009. This booklet responds to questions about current issues in reproductive technology. Available in English and Spanish.

When I Call for Help: A Pastoral Response to Domestic Violence Against Women. Tenth Anniversary Edition. Washington, DC: USCCB, 2002. A compassionate presentation on the challenges of domestic abuse, addressed to those who are abused, abusers, and the faith community. Available in English and Spanish.

USCCB Web Sites

For Your Marriage (*www.foryourmarriage.org*). Offers practical advice, information and resources for couples at all stages of marriage.

Por Tu Matrimonio (*www.portumatrimonio.org*). Spanish-language site that offers help and advice on marriage, including issues of particular concern in Hispanic communities.

Love and Life in the Divine Plan homepage (*www. usccb.org/loveandlife*). Provides links to all resources related to the pastoral letter *Marriage: Love and Life in the Divine Plan*, including the text of the letter in English and Spanish and the online version of the *Leader's Guide*.

Defense of Marriage (*www.usccb.org/defenseofmarriage*). Information and resources related to the Church's teaching on marriage as the union of one man and one woman. Also, please see *www. marriageuniqueforareason.org*.

Natural Family Planning (*www.usccb.org/prolife/ issues/nfp/index.shtml*). Information and resources for couples and those involved in natural family planning ministry.

Prayers and Blessings

Additional prayers for engaged and married couples, children and families, and events in the life of a couple or family can be found in *Catholic Household Blessings and Prayers*, revised edition (Washington, DC: USCCB, 2007).

Prayer cards for the following two prayers can also be purchased in bulk from *www.usccbpublishing.org*.

Consider ordering a quantity to hand out to the participants in your sessions.

Prayer for Families

We bless your name, O Lord,
for sending your own incarnate Son,
to become part of a family,
so that, as he lived its life,
he would experience its worries and its joys.

We ask you, Lord,
to protect and watch over this family,
so that in the strength of your grace
its members may enjoy prosperity,
possess the priceless gift of your peace,
and, as the Church alive in the home,
bear witness in this world to your glory.

We ask this through Christ our Lord.

R/. Amen.

Prayer for Married Couples

Almighty and eternal God,
You blessed the union of married couples
so that they might reflect the union of Christ
    with his Church:
look with kindness on them.
Renew their marriage covenant,
increase your love in them,
and strengthen their bond of peace
so that, with their children,
they may always rejoice in the gift of
    your blessing.

We ask this through Christ our Lord.

R/. Amen.

PART IV

———◯◯———

MARRIAGE: LOVE AND LIFE IN THE DIVINE PLAN

INTRODUCTION: THE BLESSING AND GIFT OF MARRIAGE

Blessed be the God and Father of our Lord Jesus Christ,
who has blessed us in Christ with every spiritual blessing in the heavens. (Eph 1:3)

Among the many blessings that God has showered upon us in Christ is the blessing of marriage, a gift bestowed by the Creator from the creation of the human race. His hand has inscribed the vocation to marriage in the very nature of man and woman (see Gn 1:27-28, 2:21-24).

> Father, by your plan man and woman are united,
> and married life has been established
> as the one blessing that was not forfeited by
>   original sin
> or washed away by the flood.[1]

Original Sin introduced evil and disorder into the world. As a consequence of the break with God, this first sin ruptured the original communion between man and woman. Nonetheless, the original blessing of marriage was never revoked.

Jesus Christ has not only restored the original blessing in its fullness but elevated it by making marriage between baptized Christians a sacramental sign of his own love for the Church—as we hear proclaimed in the wedding liturgy:

> Father, to reveal the plan of your love,
> you made the union of husband and wife
> an image of the covenant between you and
>   your people.
> In the fulfillment of this sacrament,
> the marriage of Christian man and woman
> is a sign of the marriage between Christ and
>   the Church.[2]

While marriage is a special blessing for Christians because of the grace of Christ, marriage is also a natural blessing and gift for everyone in all times and cultures. It is a source of blessing to the couple, to their families, and to society and includes the wondrous gift of co-creating human life. Indeed, as Pope John Paul II never tired of reminding us, the future of humanity depends on marriage and the family.[3] It is just such a conviction that has led us, the Catholic bishops of the United States, to write this pastoral letter.

We rejoice that so many couples are living in fidelity to their marital commitment. We thank them for proclaiming in their daily lives the beauty, goodness, and truth of marriage. In countless ways, both ordinary and heroic, through good times and bad, they bear witness to the gift and blessing they have received from the hand of their Creator. We are grateful, too, for all those who work with young people and engaged couples to establish good marriages, who help married couples to grow in love and strengthen their union, and who help those in crisis to resolve their problems and bring healing to their lives.

At the same time we are troubled by the fact that far too many people do not understand what it means to say that marriage—both as a natural institution and a Christian sacrament—is a blessing and gift from God. We observe, for example, that some people esteem marriage as an ideal but can be reluctant to make the actual commitment necessary to enter and sustain it. Some choose instead to live in cohabiting relationships that may or may not lead to marriage and can be detrimental to the well-being of themselves and any children.

In addition, the incidence of divorce remains high. The social sanctions and legal barriers to ending one's marriage have all but disappeared, and the negative effects of divorce on children, families, and the community have become more apparent in recent decades.

We are alarmed that a couple's responsibility to serve life by being open to children is being denied and abandoned more frequently today. Couples too often reflect a lack of understanding of the purposes of marriage. There is a loss of belief in the value of those purposes when couples readily treat, as separate choices, the decisions to get married and to have children. This indicates a mentality in which children are seen not as integral to a marriage but as optional. When children are viewed in this way, there can be damaging consequences not only for them but also for the marriage itself.

We note a disturbing trend today to view marriage as a mostly private matter, an individualistic project not related to the common good but oriented mostly to achieving personal satisfaction.

Finally, we bishops feel compelled to speak out against all attempts to redefine marriage so that it would no longer be exclusively the union of a man and a woman as God established and blessed it in the natural created order.

The opportunities and urgencies of the present moment are many and varied. Nearly thirty years ago, Pope John Paul II summoned the Church to meet a challenge that has become even more important today:

> At a moment of history in which the family is the object of numerous forces that seek to destroy it or in some way to deform it, and aware that the well-being of society and her own good are intimately tied to the good of the family, the church perceives in a more urgent and compelling way her mission of proclaiming to all people the plan of God for marriage and the family, ensuring their full vitality and human and Christian development, and thus contributing to the renewal of society and of the people of God.[4]

The task of proclamation to which the Holy Father refers is one that we bishops exercise today as teachers and pastors, specifically in this pastoral letter. We address the pastoral letter first and foremost to the Catholic faithful in the United States. We call upon them to stand against all attacks on marriage and to stand up for the meaning, dignity, and sanctity of marriage and the family. In a spirit of witness and service we also offer our message to all men and women in the hope of inspiring them to embrace this teaching.

We intend this pastoral letter to be a theological and doctrinal foundation. It can be a resource to help and encourage all those who are moving toward marriage, who are journeying in married life, and who are accompanying and assisting those who are called to the vocation of marriage.

Our pastoral letter presents those beliefs and teachings of the Catholic Church—informed by human reason and enlightened by Divine Revelation—that summarize and express God's plan for marriage. This divine plan, like the gift of marriage itself, is something we receive, not something we construct or change to fit our purposes. It is a firm foundation, a truthful guide, a trustworthy light for the way.

For all who seek to find *meaning in* their marriage will do so when they are open to accepting the transcendent *meaning of* marriage according to God's plan. Of this quest for meaning and truth, Pope Benedict XVI writes:

> All people feel the interior impulse to love authentically: love and truth never abandon them completely, because these are the vocation planted by God in the heart and mind of every human person. The search for love and truth is purified and liberated by Jesus Christ from the impoverishment that our humanity brings to it, and he reveals to us in all its fullness the initiative of love and the plan for true life that God has prepared for us.[5]

Our pastoral letter is an invitation to discover, or perhaps rediscover, the blessing given when God first established marriage as a natural institution and when Christ restored and elevated it as a sacramental sign of salvation.

PART ONE: MARRIAGE IN THE ORDER OF CREATION
The Natural Institution of Marriage

What Is Marriage?

Marriage is a lifelong partnership of the whole of life, of mutual and exclusive fidelity, established by mutual consent between a man and a woman, and ordered towards the good of the spouses and the procreation of offspring.[6] As the Second Vatican Council reminds us, marriage is not a purely human institution: "the intimate partnership of life and the love which constitutes the married state has been established by the creator and endowed by him with its own proper laws. . . . For God himself is the author of marriage."[7] Moreover, God has endowed marriage with certain essential attributes, without which marriage cannot exist as he intends.

The Church has taught through the ages that marriage is an exclusive relationship between one man and one woman. This union, once validly entered and consummated, gives rise to a bond that cannot be dissolved by the will of the spouses.[8] Marriage thus created is a faithful, privileged sphere of intimacy between the spouses that lasts until death.

Marriage is not merely a private institution, however. It is the foundation for the family, where children learn the values and virtues that will make good Christians as well as good citizens. The importance of marriage for children and for the upbringing of the next generation highlights the importance of marriage for all society.

Conjugal love, the love proper to marriage, is present in the commitment to the complete and total gift of self between husband and wife. Conjugal love establishes a unique communion of persons through the relationship of mutual self-giving and receiving between husband and wife, a relationship by which "a man leaves his father and mother and clings to his wife, and the two of them become one body [flesh]" (Gn 2:24).

The Second Vatican Council speaks about conjugal love in words of great beauty:

> The Lord, wishing to bestow special gifts of grace and divine love on married love, has restored, perfected, and elevated it. A love like that, bringing together the human and the divine, leads the partners to a free and mutual self-giving, experienced in tenderness and action, and permeating their entire lives; this love is actually developed and increased by its generous exercise.[9]

As Part Two of this pastoral letter will examine, in conjugal love one can see something of how Christ loves his Church (Eph 5:25).

Male-Female Complementarity Is Essential to Marriage

> God created man in his image,
> in the divine image he created him;
> male and female he created them. (Gn 1:27)

The two creation stories in the book of Genesis communicate two important truths about the identity of man and woman and the relationship between them. In the first account, God creates both male and female at the same time and in the divine image. This act completes creation, and God judges it to be "very good" (Gn 1:31). In this way, Sacred Scripture affirms the fundamental equality and dignity of man and woman as persons created in God's image.

The second creation account emphasizes that both sexes are necessary for God's plan. Having created Adam, God says, "It is not good for the man to be alone" (Gn 2:18). So God creates a helpmate who is suitable for him and matches him. "Helpmate" (*ezer*) is a word reserved in the Bible not for inferiors but most often for God himself, who is Israel's "helper." Indeed, after God creates all of the animals and brings them to Adam to name, it becomes clear that none of them is "the suitable partner for the man" (Gn 2:20).

Then God puts Adam under a deep sleep and, using one of his ribs, builds up a woman for him as a suitable partner or helpmate. When he sees the woman, Adam cries out in wondrous joy:

This one, at last, is bone of my bones
    and flesh of my flesh;
This one shall be called "woman" [*ishah*],
    for out of "her man" [*ish*] this one has been
        taken. (Gn 2:23)

Adam and Eve were literally made for each other. Man and woman have been made to come together in the union of marriage. The text of Genesis continues: "That is why a man leaves his father and mother and clings to his wife, and the two of them become one body [flesh]" (Gn 2:24).

Marriage, this clinging together of husband and wife as one flesh, is based on the fact that man and woman are both different and the same. They are different as male and female, but the same as human persons who are uniquely suited to be partners or helpmates for each other. The difference between man and woman, however, cannot be restricted to their bodies, as if the body could be separated from the rest of the human person. The human person is a union of body and soul as a single being. Man and woman are two different ways of being a human person.

While man and woman are different, their differences serve to relate them to each other. They are not different in a parallel way, as two lines that never meet. Man and woman do not have separate destinies. They are related to each other precisely in their differences.

The differences between male and female are complementary. Male and female are distinct bodily ways of being human, of being open to God and to one another—two distinct yet harmonizing ways of responding to the vocation to love.

While human persons are more than biological organisms, the roots of marriage can be seen in the biological fact that a man and a woman can come together as male and female in a union that has the potential for bringing forth another human person. This kind of union fills the need for the continuation of the human race. Since human beings exist at more than a biological level, however, this union has further personal and spiritual dimensions. Marriage does not exist solely for the reproduction of another member of the species, but for the creation of a communion of persons.

To form a communion of persons is the vocation of everyone. As Pope John Paul II teaches, all human persons are created in the image of God, who is a communion of love of three persons, and thus all are called to live in a communion of self-giving love: "to say that man is created in the image and likeness of God means that man is called to exist 'for' others, to become a gift."[10]

Marriage, however, is a unique communion of persons. In their intimate union as male and female, the spouses are called to exist for each other. Just as Genesis describes Eve as a helper for Adam, we can see that in marriage, a husband and wife are meant to help each other through self-giving. "In the 'unity of the two,' man and woman are called from the beginning not only to exist 'side by side' or 'together,' but they are also called *to exist mutually 'one for the other.'*"[11]

This communion of persons has the potential to bring forth human life and thus to produce the family, which is itself another kind of communion of persons and which is the origin and foundation of all human society. It is precisely the difference between man and woman that makes possible this unique communion of persons, the unique partnership of life and love that is marriage. A man and woman united in marriage as husband and wife serve as a symbol of both life and love in a way that no other relationship of human persons can.

The Two Ends or Purposes of Marriage

Marriage has two fundamental ends or purposes towards which it is oriented, namely, the good of the spouses as well as the procreation of children. Thus, the Church teaches that marriage is both unitive and procreative, and that it is inseparably both.

Unitive

Pope John Paul II's theology of the body speaks of the human body as having a spousal significance. This means that the human body by its very nature signifies that we humans are directed to relationship—that we are to seek union with others. For it is only in relationship that we achieve a true wholeness as a communion of persons. Before Eve was created, Adam was alone. His joy upon perceiving Eve indicated that with Eve he achieved the "original unity" that human nature seeks. God clearly made human beings to love and to be loved, to be in relationships wherein the act of giving oneself and receiving the other becomes complete.

In this context, the word "original" means not only that these experiences go back to the dawn of human history but, more importantly, that they are key to understanding our most basic human experiences. The experience of Adam and Eve speaks powerfully to our search not only to understand ourselves but also to love and be loved, to be in a relationship of love with a person of the opposite sex.

God established marriage so that man and woman could participate in his love and thus selflessly give themselves to each other in love. A man and a woman who by their act of consent are no longer two but one flesh (see Mt 19:6ff.) render mutual help and service to each other through an intimate union of their persons and of their actions.[12]

"My lover belongs to me and I to him" (Song 2:16; see Song 6:3). With all the dignity and simplicity of poetry, the Bride in the Song of Songs sings of the unitive meaning of married love.

"You have ravished my heart, my sister, my bride. . . . How beautiful is your love!" (Song 4:9-10). So responds the Bridegroom of the Song, overcome with the wonder of conjugal love that is extended to him by the Bride.[13] This is the love that is strong as death (see Song 8:6b).

Just as beautifully, Tobiah prays with his wife, Sarah, on their wedding night, awestruck at the mercy of the God of their fathers, that is, the God of the covenant, in bringing them together in a union of true conjugal love:

> Blessed are you, O God of our fathers;
> praised be your name forever and ever.
> Let the heavens and all your creation praise
> you forever.
> You made Adam and you gave him his wife Eve
> to be his help and support;
> and from these two the human
> race descended.
> You said, "It is not good for the man to be alone;
> let us make him a partner like himself."
> Now, Lord, you know that I take this wife
> of mine
> not because of lust,
> but for a noble purpose.
> Call down your mercy on me and on her,
> and allow us to live together to a happy
> old age. (Tb 8:5-7)

The love that is as strong as death is the love that prays and praises, caught up into divine love.[14]

Procreative

It is the nature of love to overflow, to be life-giving. Thus, it is no surprise that marriage is ordained not only to growing in love but to transmitting life: "by its very nature the institution of marriage and married love [is] ordered to the procreation and education of the offspring and it is in them that it finds its crowning glory."[15]

Married love itself is ordered to the procreation of children, for, after all, the first command given to Adam and Eve is "be fertile and multiply" (Gn 1:28). Tobiah's prayer, even as it asks for a happy and lifelong union, remembers that the human race descended from Adam and Eve. His prayer for happiness certainly includes, even if implicitly, a prayer for offspring. God indeed sends the couple seven sons (Tb 14:3) and long life (Tb 14:14). Again, in the words of the Second Vatican Council:

> Children are the supreme gift of marriage. . . . Without intending to underestimate the other ends of marriage, it must be said that true married love and the family life which flows from it have this end in view: that the spouses would cooperate generously with the love of the Creator and Savior, who through them will in due time increase and enrich his family.[16]

Children are a gift in a myriad of ways. They bring joy even in the midst of heartaches; they give added direction to the lives of their parents. Children, who are the fruit of love and meaningful commitment, are a cause of love and meaning.

It is true that some marriages will not result in procreation due to infertility, even though the couple is capable of the natural act by which procreation takes place. Indeed, this situation often comes as a surprise and can be a source of deep disappointment, anxiety, and even great suffering for a husband and wife. When such tragedy affects a marriage, a couple may be tempted to think that their union is not complete or truly blessed. This is not true. The marital union of a man and a woman is a distinctive communion of persons. An infertile couple continues to manifest this attribute.

Even when their child-bearing years have passed, a couple should continue to be life-affirming. They can do this by staying involved in the lives of young people, and especially their grandchildren, as spiritual mentors, teachers, and wisdom figures. They can also continue to be nurturing through the exercise of care for those who are needy, disabled, or pushed to the margins of society, and by their support for or participation in works of charity and justice.

How Are the Two Ends of Marriage Related?

The Church speaks of an inseparable connection between the two ends of marriage: the good of the spouses themselves as well as the procreation of children. The *Catechism of the Catholic Church* teaches that "these two meanings or values of marriage cannot be separated without altering the couple's spiritual life and compromising the goods of marriage and the future of the family."[17] This inseparability arises from the very nature of conjugal love, a love that "stands under the twofold obligation of fidelity and fecundity."[18]

Conjugal love expresses the unitive meaning of marriage in such a way as to show how this meaning is ordered toward the equally obvious procreative meaning. The unitive meaning is distorted if the procreative meaning is deliberately disavowed. Conjugal love is then diminished. This love is, by its nature, faithful, exclusive, and intended to be fecund. As Pope Paul VI says, "It is not confined wholly to the loving interchange of husband and wife; it also contrives to go beyond this to bring new life into being."[19] Without its ordering toward the procreative, the unitive meaning of marriage is undermined.

Likewise, the procreative meaning of marriage is degraded without the unitive. If someone were to view his or her spouse simply as a way of producing offspring, with no loving attentiveness to the spouse's own good or fulfillment, this would offend against the human value of the procreative meaning.

The procreative meaning of marriage involves not only the conception of children, but also their upbringing and education, including spiritual formation in the life of love. This formation can take place only within a human community formed in love. The loving communion of the spouses is the primary context in which children are both conceived and brought up in love.

The unitive and the procreative purposes are meant to be inseparable. In this way, the procreative requires the unitive, just as the unitive is ordered to the procreative. These are two connected meanings of the same reality.

We can better understand this intrinsic connection if we consider the fact that procreation is a participation in the ongoing creative activity of God. The *Catechism of the Catholic Church* states that God's creative power is not a power of force or manipulation, but a power of love.[20] It is a power of self-gift. God is eternally happy in himself because he is a loving communion of three persons. He is self-sufficient and needs nothing else to be happy. Yet he wills to share his life and happiness with creatures who would have no existence were it not for this creative self-gift. Participating in the creative work of God means participating in the self-emptying or self-giving love of God, the rendering of one's whole being into a gift. If procreation is a true participation in the creative activity of God, it is a work that is inseparable from self-gift.

In the case of marriage, the principal and original self-gift is the unitive, mutual self-gift of the spouses to each other. In their marriage promises, the spouses pledge love and fidelity for as long as they live. The transmission of life is a sublime, concrete realization of this radical self-gift between a man and a woman. The mutual married love of man and woman "becomes an image of the absolute and unfailing love with which God loves man[kind],"[21] because as mutual self-gift, it is at the same time creative self-gift. The unitive and the procreative meanings of marriage are joined because they are two aspects of the same self-giving.

Fundamental Challenges to the Nature and Purposes of Marriage

We recognize that couples face many challenges to building and sustaining a strong marriage. Conditions in contemporary society do not always support marriage. For example, many couples struggle to balance home and work responsibilities; others bear serious economic and social burdens.

Some challenges, however, are fundamental in the sense that they are directed at the very meaning and purposes of marriage. Here we want to discuss four such challenges: contraception, same-sex unions, divorce, and cohabitation.

1. Contraception

Just as there are two inseparable purposes of marriage as a whole, the same is true of the act most symbolic and expressive of the marriage as a whole, namely, the act of sexual intercourse. Church teaching speaks of an "inseparable connection, established by God, which man on his own initiative

may not break, between the unitive significance and the procreative significance which are both inherent to the marriage act."[22]

Sometimes one hears it said that as long as the marriage as a whole is open to children, each individual act of intercourse need not be. In fact, however, a marriage is only as open to procreation as each act of intercourse is, because the whole meaning of marriage is present and signified in each marital act. Each marital act signifies, embodies, and renews the original and enduring marital covenant between husband and wife. That is what makes intercourse exclusively a *marital* act. Engaging in marital intercourse is speaking the "language of the body," as Pope John Paul II calls it—a language of personal communion in complete and mutual self-donation.[23]

The spouses' mutual promise of lifelong love and fidelity provides this act with the clarity of an explicitly stated intention that enables the language of the body to be spoken. It is the intention of both spouses to cling together for life as "one flesh," in a completely mutual self-gift that gives the language of the body its voice. In each marital act, this intention is signified, or "spoken." Each marital act signifies the grateful openness to all of God's gifts. When the act signifies this grateful openness, one gives oneself completely, without shame (see Gn 2:25).

Deliberately intervening, by the use of contraceptive practices, to close off an act of intercourse to the possibility of procreation is a way of separating the unitive meaning of marriage from the procreative meaning. This is objectively wrong in and of itself and is essentially opposed to God's plan for marriage and proper human development. It makes the act of intercourse signify, or speak, something less than the unreserved self-gift intended in the marriage promises. The language of the body that is meant to express self-gift becomes mixed with another message, a contrary message—namely, the refusal to give oneself entirely. Thus the unitive meaning of that language is falsified.[24]

"By using contraception," married couples "may think that they are avoiding problems or easing tensions, that they are exerting control over their lives."[25] At the same time, they may think that they are doing nothing harmful to their marriages. In reality, the deliberate separation of the procreative and unitive meanings of marriage has the potential to damage or destroy the marriage. Also, it results in many other negative consequences, both personal and social.

Conjugal love is diminished whenever the union of a husband and wife is reduced to a means of self-gratification. The procreative capacity of male and female is dehumanized, reduced to a kind of internal biological technology that one masters and controls just like any other technology. Pope Paul VI warns against treating the sexual faculties as simply one more technology to control:

> to experience the gift of married love while respecting the laws of conception is to acknowledge that one is not the master of the sources of life but rather the minister of the design established by the Creator. Just as man does not have unlimited dominion over his body in general, so also, and with more particular reason, he has no such dominion over his specifically sexual faculties, for these are concerned by their very nature with the generation of life, of which God is the source.[26]

The procreative capacity of man and woman should not be treated as just another means of technology, as also happens with *in vitro* fertilization (IVF) or cloning. When that happens, human life itself is degraded because it becomes, more and more, something produced or manufactured in various ways, ways that will only multiply as science advances. Children begin to be seen less as gifts received in a personal communion of mutual self-giving, and increasingly as a lifestyle choice, a commodity to which all consumers are entitled. There is a true issue of the dignity of human life at stake here. In this context, the warning of Pope Paul VI seems prophetic in retrospect:

> In preserving intact the whole moral law of marriage, the Church is convinced that she is contributing to the creation of a truly human civilization. She urges man not to betray his personal responsibilities by putting all his faith in technical expedients. In this way she defends the dignity of husband and wife. . . . [and with it] "man's essential dignity."[27]

Finally, living according to God's design for love and life does not mean that married couples cannot plan their families. The principle of responsible parenthood describes the way spouses can work with God's gift of fertility. Rooted in "the objective moral order which was established by God," spouses can "recognize their own duties towards God, themselves, their families and human society" as they decide when to try to achieve a pregnancy or conclude that there are sufficiently serious reasons to justify postponing one.[28] Today, the Church is particularly blessed that viable scientific methods of natural family planning are available to support responsible parenthood.

Natural family planning (NFP) methods represent authentic family planning. They can be used both to achieve and to postpone a pregnancy. NFP makes use of periodic abstinence from sexual intercourse based upon the observation of the woman's natural signs of fertility, in order to space births or to limit the number of children when there is a serious reason to do so. NFP methods require that couples learn, accept, and live with the wonders of how God made them. This is essentially different from contraception.

Openness to procreation in the marital act involves "acknowledg[ing] that one is not the master of the sources of life."[29] Using the technology of contraception is an attempt at such mastery. By contrast, couples using methods of NFP do nothing to alter the conjugal act. Rather, they abstain from conjugal relations during the portion of the woman's menstrual cycle when conception is most likely. This practice fosters in couples an attitude of respect and wonder in the face of human life, which is sacred. It also fosters profound respect for one's spouse, which is necessary for the mutual enjoyment of authentic intimacy.

As Pope John Paul II observes, any couple who tries to live out this openness to procreation will find that it requires a sacrificial love.[30] At certain difficult times in life, the procreative meaning of marriage may seem to be at odds with the unitive meaning. Though this can in fact never be the case, preserving unity may in some cases require a considerable sacrifice by couples. They should take heart from St. Paul's assurance that God will not test us beyond what we can endure: "God is faithful and will not let you be tried beyond your strength; but with the trial he will also provide a way out, so that you may be able to bear it" (1 Cor 10:13).

2. Same-Sex Unions

One of the most troubling developments in contemporary culture is the proposition that persons of the same sex can "marry." This proposal attempts to redefine the nature of marriage and the family and, as a result, harms both the intrinsic dignity of every human person and the common good of society.

Marriage is a unique union, a relationship different from all others. It is the permanent bond between one man and one woman whose two-in-one-flesh communion of persons is an indispensable good at the heart of every family and every society. Same-sex unions are incapable of realizing this specific communion of persons. Therefore, attempting to redefine marriage to include such relationships empties the term of its meaning, for it excludes the essential complementarity between man and woman, treating sexual difference as if it were irrelevant to what marriage is.

Male-female complementarity is intrinsic to marriage. It is naturally ordered toward authentic union and the generation of new life. Children are meant to be the gift of the permanent and exclusive union of a husband and a wife. A child is meant to have a mother and a father. The true nature of marriage, lived in openness to life, is a witness to the precious gift of the child and to the unique roles of a mother and father. Same-sex unions are incapable of such a witness. Consequently, making them equivalent to marriage disregards the very nature of marriage.[31]

Jesus teaches that marriage is between a man and a woman. "Have you not read that from the beginning the Creator 'made them male and female' . . . For this reason a man shall leave his father and mother and be joined to his wife, and the two shall become one flesh" (Mt 19:4-6).

By attempting to redefine marriage to include or be made analogous with homosexual partnerships, society is stating that the permanent union of husband and wife, the unique pattern of spousal and familial love, and the generation of new life are now only of relative importance rather than being fundamental to the existence and well-being of society as a whole.

Today, advocacy for the legal recognition of various same-sex relationships is often equated with non-discrimination, fairness, equality, and civil rights. However, it is not unjust to oppose legal recognition of same-sex unions, because marriage and same-sex unions are essentially different realities. "The denial of the social and legal status of marriage to forms of cohabitation that are not and cannot be marital is not opposed to justice; on the contrary, justice requires it."[32] To promote and protect marriage as the union of one man and one woman is itself a matter of justice. In fact, it would be a grave injustice if the state ignored the unique and proper place of husbands and wives, the place of mothers and fathers, and especially the rights of children, who deserve from society clear guidance as they grow to sexual maturity. Indeed, without this protection the state would, in effect, *intentionally* deprive children of the right to a mother and father.

The Church upholds the human dignity of homosexual persons, who are to "be accepted with respect, compassion, and sensitivity."[33] She also encourages all persons to have chaste friendships. "Chastity is expressed notably in *friendship with one's neighbor.* Whether it develops between persons of the same or opposite sex, friendship represents a great good for all."[34]

At the same time, the Church teaches that homosexual acts "are contrary to the natural law. They close the sexual act to the gift of life. They do not proceed from a genuine affective and sexual complementarity. Under no circumstances can they be approved."[35]

Basic human rights must be afforded to all people. This can and should be done without sacrificing the bedrock of society that is marriage and the family and without violating the religious liberty of persons and institutions.

The legal recognition of same-sex unions poses a multifaceted threat to the very fabric of society, striking at the source from which society and culture come and which they are meant to serve. Such recognition affects all people, married and non-married: not only at the fundamental levels of the good of the spouses, the good of children, the intrinsic dignity of every human person, and the common good, but also at the levels of education, cultural imagination and influence, and religious freedom.

3. Divorce

By its very nature, marriage is meant to be a life-long covenantal union. Fidelity until death is what couples aspire to and what they promise to each other. Divorce, therefore, "claims to break the contract, to which the spouses freely consented, to live with each other till death."[36] Moreover, Jesus himself teaches that divorce does not accord with the binding nature of marriage as intended by the Creator (see Mt 19:3-9).

Conflict, quarrels, and misunderstandings can be found in all marriages. They reflect the impact of Original Sin, which "disrupted the original communion of man and woman."[37] They also reflect modern stresses upon marriage: the conflict between work and home, economic hardships, and social expectations.

Nevertheless, God's plan for marriage persists, and he continues to offer mercy and healing grace. We bishops urge couples in crisis to turn to the Lord for help. We also encourage them to make use of the many resources, including programs and ministries offered by the Church, that can help to save marriages, even those in serious difficulty.

In some cases, divorce may be the only solution to a morally unacceptable situation. A specific example is a home where the safety of a spouse and children is at risk. As the Catholic bishops of the United States, we reiterate what we said in our pastoral message on domestic violence, *When I Call for Help*, namely, that no one in a marriage is obliged to maintain common living with an abusing spouse.[38] We want to assure people who are caught in the tragedy of an abusive marriage that the Church is committed to offering them support and assistance.

We understand the pain of those for whom divorce seemed the only recourse. We urge them to make frequent use of the sacraments, especially the Sacraments of Holy Eucharist and Reconciliation. We also offer encouragement to those who have divorced and remarried civilly. Although the Church cannot recognize such subsequent unions as valid marriages, she hopes that people in this situation will participate in parish life and attend the Sunday Eucharist, even without receiving the Sacrament.

We encourage divorced persons who wish to marry in the Catholic Church to seek counsel about the options that exist to remedy their situation, including the suitability of a declaration of nullity when there is no longer any hope of reconciliation of the spouses. Such a declaration is a finding by a church tribunal, or court, that no valid marriage bond was formed because the requirements for valid consent were not met at the time of the wedding. If a declaration of nullity is granted, and there are no other restrictions, both parties are free to marry in the Catholic Church. Although the purpose of this canonical process is to determine whether or not a marriage bond truly existed, nonetheless, the process can often result in healing and closure to a painful part of one's past.

4. Living Together Without Marriage

Today many couples are living together in a sexual relationship without the benefit of marriage. Many cohabiting couples believe that their desire for each other justifies the sexual relationship. This belief reflects a misunderstanding of the natural purpose of human sexual intercourse, which can only be realized in the permanent commitment of marriage. Sexual intercourse is meant to express the total and unrestricted gift of self that takes place in married love. To have sexual intercourse outside the covenant of marriage is gravely immoral because it communicates physically the gift of oneself to another when, at the same time, one is not willing or able to make a total and permanent commitment.

Couples offer various reasons for cohabiting, ranging from economics to convenience. Frequently, they have accepted the widespread societal belief that premarital cohabitation is a prudent way to determine whether they are truly compatible. They believe they need a trial period before proceeding to the lifelong commitment of marriage.

Social science research, however, finds that cohabitation has no positive effects on a marriage.[39] In some cases, cohabitation can in fact harm a couple's chances for a stable marriage. More importantly, though, cohabitation "involves the serious sin of fornication. It does not conform to God's plan for marriage and is always wrong and objectively sinful."[40]

Clearly, there is no substitute for the binding lifelong commitment of marriage, and by definition, there is certainly no way to "try it out." Only the public and legal commitment of marriage expresses the complete gift of self that is the basis of marriage.[41] To refuse the full commitment of marriage expresses something distinctly less than the unconditional trust required of complete self-giving.[42] At the heart of cohabitation lies a reluctance or refusal to make a public, permanent commitment. Young people need to develop the virtue required for sustaining such a lofty commitment.

Cohabitation can also have a negative impact on children. Many cohabiting couples bring children into the relationship, or children result from the relationship. The unstable nature of cohabitation puts these children at risk. With regard to the good of the children, a stable marriage between the parents is "the most human and humanizing context for welcoming children, the context which most readily provides emotional security and guarantees greater unity and continuity in the process of social integration and education."[43] The findings of the social sciences confirm that the best environment for raising children is a stable home provided by the marriage of their parents.[44]

Just as families render an invaluable service to society, society has a reciprocal obligation to protect and support families. The Second Vatican Council affirms that the well-being of society is closely tied to healthy marriages and families.[45] The *Catechism of the Catholic Church* explains:

> The family is the *original cell of social life*. It is the natural society in which husband and wife are called to give themselves in love and in the gift of life. Authority, stability, and a life of relationships within the family constitute the foundations for freedom, security, and fraternity within society.[46]

PART TWO: MARRIAGE IN THE ORDER OF THE NEW CREATION
The Sacrament of Matrimony

In Part One, we discussed why and how the natural institution of marriage is a gift and blessing. Now, in Part Two, we will consider what it means to say that this natural institution has been raised by Christ to the dignity of a sacrament for Christians. If marriage is crucial to society on a natural level, it is also crucial to the Church on the supernatural level.

Married Life Affected by Original Sin

While marriage has remained the good gift that God created it to be, and so has not been a blessing forfeited because of the Fall, Original Sin has had grave consequences for married life. Because men and women became wounded by sin, marriage has become distorted. In the words of the *Catechism of the Catholic Church,*

> As a break with God, the first sin had for its first consequence the rupture of the original communion between man and woman. Their relations were distorted by mutual recriminations; their mutual attraction, the Creator's own gift, changed into a relationship of domination and lust; and the beautiful vocation of man and woman to be fruitful, multiply, and subdue the earth was burdened by the pain of childbirth and the toil of work.[47]

Marriage Restored in Christ

Through Baptism, men and women are transformed, by the power of the Holy Spirit, into a new creation in Christ.[48] This new life in the Holy Spirit heals men and women from sin and elevates them to share in God's very own divine life. It is within this new Christian context that Jesus has raised marriage between the baptized to the dignity of a sacrament.[49] He heals marriage and restores it to its original purity of permanent self-giving in one flesh (see Mt 19:6).

In restoring to marriage its original meaning and beauty, Jesus proclaims what the Creator meant marriage to be "in the beginning." He does so because marriage will be made into the visible embodiment of his love for the Church. In his espousal of the Church as his Bride, he fulfills and elevates marriage. He reveals his own love "to the end" (Jn 13:1) as the purest and deepest love, the perfection of all love. In doing this he reveals the deepest meaning of all marital love: self-giving love modeled on God's inner life and love.

In marriage a man and a woman are united with each other, and the two become one flesh, so that they each love the other as they love themselves and cherish each other's bodies as their own. This union is an image of the relationship between Christ and his Church:

> He who loves his wife loves himself. For no one hates his own flesh but rather nourishes and

cherishes it, even as Christ does the church, because we are members of his body.

> "For this reason a man shall leave [his]
> father and [his] mother
> and be joined to his wife,
> and the two shall become one flesh."

This is a great mystery, but I speak in reference to Christ and the church. (Eph 5:28-32)

The Church Fathers expressed this truth when they described the relationship between Adam and Eve as a "type," or mysterious foreshadowing, of the relationship between Christ and the Church. The kind of relationship of love that is foreshadowed in the relationship between Adam and Eve is fulfilled in the relationship between Christ and his Church.

The Sacrament of Matrimony renews the natural institution of marriage and elevates it so that it shares in a love larger than itself. Marriage, then, is nothing less than a participation in the covenant between Christ and the Church. In the words of the Second Vatican Council,

> Spouses, therefore, are fortified and, as it were, consecrated for the duties and dignity of their state by [this] special sacrament; fulfilling their conjugal and family role by virtue of this sacrament, spouses are penetrated with the spirit of Christ and their whole life is suffused by faith, hope and charity; thus they increasingly further their own perfection and their mutual sanctification, and together they render glory to God.[50]

Because the call of Adam and Eve to become one flesh is realized on a more profound level in the creation of the Church as Christ's Bride, one can only see the depth of the meaning of marriage in relation to Christ and his love for the Church as his Bride. Marriage is a call to give oneself to one's spouse as fully as Christ gave himself to the Church. The natural meaning of marriage as an exchange of self-giving is not replaced, but fulfilled and raised to a higher level.

Christian Marriage as a Sacrament

Marriage is one of the Church's "mysteries," or sacraments. The *Catechism of the Catholic Church* puts it this way: "Christian marriage . . . becomes an efficacious sign, the sacrament of the covenant of Christ and the Church."[51] An "efficacious sign" is one that does not merely symbolize or signify something, but actually makes present what it signifies. Marriage signifies and makes present to baptized spouses the love of Christ by which he formed the Church as his spouse: "just as of old God encountered his people in a covenant of love and fidelity, so our Savior, the spouse of the church, now encounters Christian spouses through the sacrament of marriage."[52]

By using the image of the relationship between bridegroom and bride to explain the relationship between Christ and the Church, the Scriptures are appealing to a natural human relationship that is already well known. All of us know something about the depth, the intimacy, and the beauty of the gift of self that occurs in the marriage of husband and wife. The Scriptures also show us, however, that Christ's love for the Church surpasses natural human love. Christ's love for the Church is a love of complete self-giving. This love is most completely expressed by his death on the Cross. Christian marriage aspires not only to natural human love, but to Christ's love for the Church:

> Husbands, love your wives, even as Christ loved the church and handed himself over for her to sanctify her, cleansing her by the bath of water with the word, that he might present to himself the church in splendor, without spot or wrinkle or any such thing, that she might be holy and without blemish. (Eph 5:25-27)

Christian spouses are called to this imitation of Christ, an imitation that is possible only because, in the Sacrament of Matrimony, the couple receives a participation in his love. As a sacrament, marriage signifies and makes present in the couple Christ's total self-gift of love. Their mutual gift of self, conferred in their promises of fidelity and love *to the end*, becomes a participation in the *love to the end* by which Christ gave himself to the Church as to a Spouse (see Jn 13:1).

The baptized spouses are the ministers of the Sacrament of Matrimony. In addition, for marriages that are celebrated within the Latin Catholic Church, canonical form requires, among other things, that an authorized bishop, priest, or deacon ask for and receive the spouses' consent as the Church's official witness of the marriage celebration. For marriages of members of the Eastern Catholic Churches, the assistance and blessing of an authorized bishop or priest is required.[53] The Holy Spirit binds the spouses together through their exchange of promises in a bond of love and fidelity unto death. Their marriage covenant becomes a participation in the unbreakable covenant between Christ the Bridegroom and his Bride, the Church. The same love that defines the Church now defines the communion between the two spouses: "authentic married love is caught up into divine love and is directed and enriched by the redemptive power of Christ and the salvific action of the church."[54]

When Christian couples receive the grace of the Sacrament of Matrimony,

> Christ dwells with them, gives them the strength to take up their crosses and so follow him, to rise again after they have fallen, to forgive one another, to bear one another's burdens, to "be subject to one another out of reverence for Christ," and to love one another with supernatural, tender, and fruitful love.[55]

By the power of the Holy Spirit, spouses become willing to do the acts and courtesies of love toward each other, regardless of the feelings of the moment. They are formed by the self-giving love of Christ for his Church as his Bride, and so they are enabled to perform acts of self-giving love to the benefit of themselves, their families, and the whole Church. The Sacrament of Matrimony, like the Sacrament of Holy Orders, is a sacrament "directed toward the salvation of others; if [these sacraments] contribute as well to personal salvation, it is through service to others that they do so."[56] Those who receive these sacraments are given a special consecration in Christ's name to carry out the duties of their particular state in life.

The imitation of the love of Christ for the Church also calls for a healing of the relationship between man and woman. This should not be a one-sided subjection of the wife to the husband, but rather a mutual subjection of husband and wife. St. Paul did indeed speak in a way that, according to Pope John Paul II, was "profoundly rooted in the customs and religious tradition of the time": "wives should be subordinate to their husbands as to the Lord" (Eph 5:22). The Holy Father explains, however, that this saying must "be understood and carried out in a new way," that is, in light of what St. Paul said immediately before: "be subordinate to one another out of reverence for Christ" (Eph 5:21). He emphasizes that this is something new, "an innovation of the Gospel," that has challenged and will continue to challenge the succeeding generations after St. Paul.[57]

Marriage as a Reflection of the Life of the Trinity

Throughout history God has shown us his selfless love. In espousing himself to the Church in sacrificial, life-giving love, Christ reveals the Father's love in the power of the Holy Spirit. He shows us the inner life of the Holy Trinity, a communion of persons, Father, Son, and Holy Spirit. The Church herself is a communion of persons that shares in God's Trinitarian life and love.

> The mystery of the Most Holy Trinity is the central mystery of Christian faith and life. It is the mystery of God in himself. It is therefore the source of all the other mysteries of faith, the light that enlightens them. It is the most fundamental and essential teaching in the "hierarchy of the truths of faith."[58]

Through the Sacrament of Matrimony, married love not only is modeled on Trinitarian love but also participates in it. Like all sacraments, Matrimony draws believers more deeply into the Trinitarian life of God. It was not until the Father sent his Son into the world as man, and the subsequent outpouring of the Holy Spirit, that the full identity of God as a Trinity of Persons was revealed. This

Revelation not only allowed humankind to come to a definitive knowledge of God—since the mystery of the Trinity is the source of all the other mysteries, the revelation of this mystery sheds light on all the rest. This includes both the mystery that human beings are created in the image and likeness of God and the mystery that is marriage and family life.

As we learn from the mystery of the Trinity, to be in the image and likeness of God is not simply to have intelligence and free will, but also to live in a communion of love. From all eternity the Father begets his Son in the love of the Spirit. In the begetting of the Son, the Father gives himself entirely over to the Son in the love of the Holy Spirit. The Son, having been begotten of the Father, perfectly returns that love by giving himself entirely over to the Father in the same Spirit of love. It is because he is begotten of the Father, and loves the Father in the same Spirit, that he is called Son. The Holy Spirit is then acknowledged as the mutual love of the Father for his Son and of the Son for his Father. This is why the Spirit is known as the gift of love.

Here one can see that the Father, the Son, and the Holy Spirit give themselves entirely to one another in a life-giving exchange of love. Thus, the Trinity is a loving and life-giving communion of equal Persons. The one God is the loving interrelationship of the Father, the Son, and the Holy Spirit.

To be created in the image and likeness of God means, therefore, that human beings reflect not the life of a solitary deity, but the communal life of the Trinity. Human beings were created not to live solitary lives, but to live in communion with God and with one another, a communion that is both life-giving and loving. "The divine image is present in every man. It shines forth in the communion of persons, in the likeness of the unity of the divine persons among themselves."[59]

On a basic level this is witnessed in the social nature of human beings. We live in societies for the mutual benefit of all. "All men are called to the same end: God himself. There is a certain resemblance between the unity of the divine persons and the fraternity that men are to establish among themselves in truth and love. Love of neighbor is inseparable from love of God."[60] In the smaller community of the married couple and their family, the image of the Trinity can be seen even more clearly. Here are two ways to see the Trinitarian image in marriage and family life.

First, like the Persons of the Trinity, marriage is a communion of love between co-equal persons, beginning with that between husband and wife and then extending to all the members of the family. Pope John Paul II teaches, "The family, which is founded and given life by love, is a community of persons: of husband and wife, of parents and children, of relatives."[61]

This communion of life-giving love is witnessed within the life of the family, where parents and children, brothers and sisters, grandparents and relatives are called to live in loving harmony with one another and to provide mutual support to one another. The *Catechism of the Catholic Church* teaches that "the Christian family is a communion of persons, a sign and image of the communion of the Father and the Son in the Holy Spirit."[62]

These relations among the persons in communion simultaneously distinguish them from one another and unite them to one another. For example, the Father is only the Father in relation to the Son and the Holy Spirit. Therefore, just as the Father, the Son, and the Holy Spirit are distinctly who they are only in relation to one another, so a man and a woman are distinctly who they are as husband and wife only in relation to one another. At the same time, in a way analogous to the relations among Father, Son, and Holy Spirit, which unites the three persons as one God, the interrelationship of the husband and wife make them one as a married couple.

The Trinitarian image in marriage and family life can be seen in a second way. Just as the Trinity of persons is a life-giving communion of love both in relationship to one another and to the whole of creation, so a married couple shares in this life-giving communion of love by together procreating children in the conjugal act of love. For St. Thomas Aquinas, while angels are, strictly speaking, higher than human beings by nature, the ability to procreate in love makes human beings, at least in one way, more in the image and likeness of God than the angels, who are unable to procreate. In human beings one finds "a certain imitation of God, consisting in the fact that man proceeds from man, as God proceeds from God."[63]

The Family as Domestic Church

The Christian family is a communion of persons, a sign and image of the communion of the Father and the Son in the Holy Spirit. In the procreation and education of children it reflects the Father's work of creation. It is called to partake of the prayer and sacrifice of Christ. Daily prayer and the reading of the Word of God strengthen it in charity. The Christian family has an evangelizing and missionary task.[64]

Although the Son of God was conceived in the womb of the Virgin Mary, becoming man by the power of the Holy Spirit, he was nonetheless born into a genuine human family. While Mary was his true mother, Joseph, as her husband, was the father of Jesus in the eyes of the law. It would be in living with Mary and Joseph that Jesus would learn to pray to his heavenly Father, to read and study the Scriptures, and in general to live as a devout Jewish man. With his family Jesus would attend the local synagogue and make the annual pilgrimage to Jerusalem for Passover. By being obedient to Mary and Joseph, "Jesus advanced [in] wisdom and age and favor before God and man" (Lk 2:52). It is within the context of his family that Jesus would come to know as man the will of his heavenly Father, who had sent him into the world to be its Savior and Redeemer. In contemplating the Jewish family of Joseph, Mary, and Jesus, people today can understand how this Holy Family is indeed the model and source of inspiration for all Christian families.

From the earliest days of the Church, entire families and households found salvation in Jesus. Cornelius, the first Gentile Christian, was told by an angel to send for Peter so that "all your household will be saved" (Acts 11:14). Paul and Silas preached the Gospel to their former jailer and his household. "Then he and all his family were baptized at once" (Acts 16:33). In Corinth, "Crispus, the synagogue official, came to believe in the Lord along with his entire household" (Acts 18:8). The *Catechism of the Catholic Church* states, "These families who became believers were islands of Christian life in an unbelieving world."[65] As the first Christian families were islands of faith in their time, so Catholic families today are called to be beacons of faith, "centers of living, radiant faith."[66]

Through the Sacrament of Matrimony, Christian couples are configured to Christ's love for the Church. Because of this participation in the love of Christ, the communion of persons formed by the married couple and their family is a kind of microcosm of the Church. For this reason, the Second Vatican Council employs the ancient expression "domestic church," *ecclesia domestica*, to describe the nature of the Christian family.[67] The family is called a "domestic church" because it is a small communion of persons that both draws its sustenance from the larger communion that is the whole Body of Christ, the Church, and also reflects the life of the Church so as to provide a kind of summary of it.

Pope John Paul II states, "The Christian family constitutes a specific revelation and realization of ecclesial communion, and for this reason . . . it can and should be called a *domestic church*."[68] As the Church is a community of faith, hope, and love, so the Christian family, as the domestic church, is called to be a community of faith, hope, and love. Through this faith, hope, and love, Jesus, by the power of his Holy Spirit, abides within each Christian family, as he does within the whole Church, and pours out the love of his Father within it. Every marriage between Christians gives rise to a domestic church, though marriages between two Catholics most fully reflect the life of the Church, because ordinarily only Catholic couples can fully participate in the sacraments of the Church, including the Eucharist.[69]

While all members of the family are called to live out the foundational Christian virtues, fathers and mothers have a special responsibility for fostering these virtues within their children. They are the first to proclaim the faith to their children. They are responsible for nurturing the vocation of each child, showing by example how to live the married life, and taking special care if a child might be called to priesthood or consecrated life.[70]

Not only do parents present their children for Baptism, but, having done so, they become the first evangelizers and teachers of the faith.[71] They evangelize by teaching their children to pray and by praying with them. They bring their children to Mass and teach them biblical stories. They show them how to obey God's commandments and to live a Christian life of holiness. Catholic schools, religious education programs, and Catholic homeschooling resources can help parents fulfill these responsibilities.

Cooperating together, with the help of the Holy Spirit, parents nurture the virtues within each of their children and within their family as a whole—charity, joy, peace, patience, kindness, generosity, faithfulness, gentleness, and self-control (see Gal 5:22-23). The *Catechism of the Catholic Church*, quoting the Second Vatican Council, emphasizes that the family, as a domestic church, receives its strength and life by participating in the life and worship of the larger Church of which it is a part:

It is here [within the domestic church] that the father of the family, the mother, children, and all members of the family exercise the *priesthood of the baptized* in a privileged way "by the reception of the sacraments, prayer and thanksgiving, the witness of a holy life, and self-denial and active charity" (LG, no. 10). Thus the home is the first school of Christian life and "a school for human enrichment" (GS, no. 52). Here one learns endurance and the joy of work, fraternal love, generous—even repeated—forgiveness, and above all divine worship in prayer and the offering of one's life.[72]

A family matures as a domestic church as it ever more deeply immerses itself within the life of the Church. This especially means that fathers and mothers, by their example and teaching, help their children come to an appreciation of the need for continual conversion and repentance from sin, encouraging a love for and participation in the Sacrament of Reconciliation.

Moreover, since it is Christ's presence within the family that truly makes it a domestic church, their participation in the Eucharist, especially the Sunday Eucharist, is particularly important. In the Eucharist, the family joins itself to Jesus' sacrifice to the Father for the forgiveness of sins. Furthermore, it is in receiving Holy Communion that the members of the family are most fully united to the living and glorious Christ and so to one another and to their brothers and sisters throughout the world. It is here, in the risen and Eucharistic Christ, that spouses, parents, and children express and nurture most fully the love of the Father and the bond of the Spirit.

Although Christian spouses in a mixed marriage (that is, between a Catholic and a baptized person who is not Catholic) do not ordinarily share the Eucharist,[73] they are called to "give witness to the universality of God's love which overcomes all division."[74]

These families may experience the wounds of Christian division, yet they can also contribute to healing those wounds. When the two spouses live together in peace, they provide a reminder to all Christians that progress toward the unity for which Christ prayed is possible. Mixed marriages can, therefore, make an important contribution towards Christian unity. This is especially true "when spouses are faithful to their religious duties. Their common baptism and the dynamism of grace provide the spouses in these marriages with the basis and motivation for expressing their unity in the sphere of moral and spiritual values."[75]

Catholics sometimes enter into valid marriages with persons of other religions that do not profess faith in Christ. Because such marriages may make more difficult a Catholic's perseverance in the faith, the Catholic party is required, after much discernment with his or her intended spouse as to the wisdom of their marrying, to obtain a dispensation to be married in the Church. Such a marriage to a non-baptized person is not a sacrament—although parties do commit to fidelity, permanence, and openness to children.

It is important to recognize the religious and cultural pressures that sometimes make it difficult for the Catholic party to share his or her faith with the children. The Catholic party needs to take seriously the obligations imposed by faith, especially in regard to the religious upbringing of children. The Church requires the Catholic party to be faithful to his or her faith and to "promise to do all in his or her power"[76] to have the children baptized and raised in the Catholic faith. The non-Catholic spouse is "to be informed at an appropriate time about the promises which the Catholic party is to make, in such a way that it is certain that he or she is truly aware of the promise and obligation of the Catholic party."[77]

In the United States, religiously mixed marriages have become increasingly common. While recognizing that other faith communities hold marriage as a sacred institution that contributes to the building of civilization, the Catholic Church also cautions that these unions face particular challenges that must be met with realism and reliance on the grace of God.

Marriage as a Vocation

God who created man out of love also calls him to love—the fundamental and innate vocation of every human being.[78]

The Church teaches that marriage is an authentic vocation, or divine call. As a vocation, marriage is just as necessary and valuable to the Church as other vocations. For this reason, all of us should pray that men and women will enter into marriage with the proper understanding and motivation and that they will live it generously and joyfully.

As with every vocation, marriage must be understood within the primary vocation to love, because humanity "is created in the image and likeness of God who is himself love."[79] In Baptism, God calls the faithful to grow in love. This vocation to love, in imitation of God's infinite love, is also a vocation to grow in holiness, for greater participation in God's love necessarily entails a greater participation in God's holiness. The Second Vatican Council teaches that "all the faithful, whatever their condition or state are called by the Lord—each in his or her own way—to that perfect holiness by which the Father himself is perfect."[80] Within this universal vocation to holiness, God calls some men to the priesthood or to the diaconate, other men and women to the consecrated life. For the vast majority of men and women, however, God places this universal vocation to holiness within the specific vocation of marriage. Those whose circumstances in life do not include marriage, ordination, or consecration are nonetheless also called to discern and make a personal gift of self in how they live a Christian life.

How do men and women discern a call to marriage? Discernment of and preparation for marriage begins early in life. *Familiaris Consortio* identifies three stages of marriage preparation: remote, proximate, and immediate.[81] *Remote* preparation occurs early in life, as children experience the love and care of married parents and begin to learn the values and virtues that will form their character. *Proximate* preparation begins around puberty and involves a more specific preparation for the sacraments, including an understanding of healthy relationships, sexuality, the virtue of chastity, and responsible parenthood.

By the time of *immediate* preparation, the couple has developed a conviction that God is calling them to marriage with a particular person. Prayer, especially for the guidance of the Holy Spirit, and the help of wise mentors are crucial in this discernment process. Discernment also involves an honest assessment of qualities that are foundational for the marriage. These include an ability to make and keep a commitment, the desire for a lifelong, faithful relationship, and openness to children. The couple will also want to reflect on the values they share, their ability to communicate, and agreement on significant issues.

The marital vocation is not a private or merely personal affair. Yes, marriage is a deeply personal union and relationship, but it is also for the good of the Church and the entire community. The Second Vatican Council teaches that "the well-being of the individual person and of both human and Christian society is closely bound up with the healthy state of marriage and the family."[82] As a vocation, or call from God, marriage has a public and ecclesial status within the Church. Catholic spouses ordinarily exchange marital consent within a church setting, before a priest or deacon.[83] The living-out of marriage takes place within the whole Body of Christ, which it serves and in which it finds nourishment.

Moreover, the state and the secular community officially recognize a couple's marital and familial status and are obliged to help support and sustain it. The ecclesial and public nature of marriage and family life is what keeps marriages and families from becoming isolated. Marriage and families are compelled, by their very nature, to contribute to the life of the Church and to the broader needs of society.

Growth in Christian Marriage

On their wedding day, the couple says a definitive "yes" to their vocation of marriage. Then the real work of marriage begins. For the remainder of their married lives, the couple is challenged to grow, through grace, into what they already are: that is, an image of Christ's love for his Church.[84]

"Become what you are!"[85] might be a great exhortation to newly married couples, especially given the strong tendency nowadays to reduce the love of the marriage bond to only a feeling, perhaps the romantic love of courtship and honeymoon. When that feeling dries up, it may seem to them that they have nothing left and that they have failed.

It is at these very times, however, that their vocation as spouses calls them to go further, to "become what they are," members of a marital communion defined by the unbreakable spousal love of Christ for his Church. While husbands and wives can cling to the unconditional promise that they made at their wedding as a source of grace, this will require persistent effort. Maintaining the common courtesies—persevering in fidelity, kindness, communication, and mutual assistance—can become a deep expression of conjugal charity. It means growing in a love that is far deeper than a romantic feeling.

That growth will be the occasion of admiration and gratitude for the good Christian example of the other spouse and for the always undeserved gift of love. In this admiration and gratitude for the enduring and faithful love of one's spouse, one can see Christ, who loved to the end. One can also recognize Christ at work in oneself as a spouse.

What about the physical expression of married love? Married couples tell us that at certain times in life marital intercourse does not seem as satisfying as it once seemed to be, and couples in this situation can come to think of themselves as having failed in the one thing that our secular culture tells us is essential. It may seem foolish or dreary to persist in a marriage that has come to seem unfulfilling. It is the consumerist-oriented version of sex, however, that is empty and inevitably unfulfilling, and that ultimately deadens sexual life.

Human beings attain their deepest fulfillment only by participation in the divine life of the Trinity, which comes through participation in the self-giving love pouring out of the pierced heart of Christ on the Cross. This fulfillment is exactly what the Sacrament of Matrimony offers.

The clarity of a promise of love to the end makes it possible for the spouses, in Christ, to achieve an intimacy where there is trust instead of shame. Leaving behind the lustful, self-centered pleasures of our culture, one can journey, in Christ, towards the discovery of an intimacy that is deeply satisfying because it is a participation in the intimate self-giving of Christ.

Growth in the Virtues

There is another way to look at growth in marriage: namely, as growth in virtue. As a couple grows in virtue, they grow in holiness. In other words, the couple acquires, by prayer and discipline, those interior qualities that open them to God's love and allow them to share in his love more deeply. Couples instinctively understand this when they speak about their marriage being a means of leading each other to heaven.

The vocation of marriage, like other vocations, is the living out of the theological virtues of faith, hope, and charity—those foundational virtues that each person receives from the Holy Spirit at Baptism and through which we all become holy. This means that a husband and wife are called to live their marriage in faith—faith in Jesus as their Lord and Savior and in accordance with the Church's teaching. They are to foster this gospel faith among themselves and within their children through their teaching and example.[86]

Likewise, they live in hope of God's kindness, mercy, and generosity. In the midst of the inevitable trials and hardships, they trust that God is graciously watching over them and their family. They trust that the Father's love will never abandon them, but that, in union with Jesus, they will always remain in his presence.

Faith and hope find their fullest expression in love—love of God and love of neighbor. The call to love reaches beyond the home to the extended family, the neighborhood, and the larger community. This marital and familial love finds its complete expression, following the example of Jesus himself, in a willingness to sacrifice oneself in everyday situations for one's spouse and children. There is no greater love within a marriage and a family than for the spouses and children to lay down their lives for one another. This is the heart of the vocation of marriage, the heart of the call to become holy.

Love in the Sacrament of Matrimony includes all the virtues, and each specific virtue is a manifestation of love. A holy marriage, one that is a communion of persons and a sign of God's love, is made up of many virtues that are acquired by human effort.

Rooted in the theological virtues, a couple must also grow in the principal moral virtues. These include prudence, justice, fortitude, and temperance. All the other virtues are grouped around these four. Practicing the moral virtues draws us ever more deeply into God's love through the Holy Spirit, with the result that we habitually manifest his love in our daily lives.

Chastity and *gratitude* are two virtues that are sometimes overlooked in relation to married life. These should be practiced in both natural and sacramental marriages.

Chastity

Everyone is called to chastity, whether married or not. The virtue of chastity is traditionally considered an expression of the virtue of temperance, which enables one to enjoy various kinds of pleasures when it is good and appropriate to do so, and to reject certain pleasures when it is not. Chastity is specifically concerned with the proper disposition of sexual desire. It refers to the peaceful integration of sexual thoughts, feelings, and desires.

Learning to live chastely is part of learning how to use one's freedom well. The *Catechism of the Catholic Church* teaches, "Chastity includes an *apprenticeship in self-mastery* which is a training in human freedom. The alternative is clear: either man governs his passions and finds peace, or he lets himself become dominated by them and becomes unhappy."[87]

Chastity will be lived somewhat differently depending on the circumstances of one's life. Single people, consecrated religious, and priests experience chastity differently from married persons. In fact, some people are surprised that married persons are called to chastity. They confuse chastity with celibacy or sexual abstinence, but marital chastity has a distinct meaning.

Married people are called to love with conjugal chastity. That is, their love is to be total, faithful, exclusive, and open to life.[88] Conjugal love merges "the human and the divine," leading the "partners to a free and mutual self-giving."[89] The practice of marital chastity ensures that both husband and wife will strive to live as a gift of self, one to the other, generously. In other words, marital chastity protects a great good: the communion of persons and the procreative purposes of marriage.

In this pastoral letter, we have already discussed how contraception threatens marital chastity. Other threats to marital chastity abound. In the workplace, men and women deal with boundary issues as they form professional relationships and personal friendships. Military deployments can strain marriages as they separate spouses for long periods of time.

Pornography, particularly Internet pornography, is a serious threat to marital chastity and is gravely immoral. The Internet has made pornography readily accessible within the privacy of one's home. Using pornography can quickly become an addiction that erodes trust and intimacy between husband and wife and, in some cases, leads to the breakup of the common life of the spouses.

A truly serious violation of marital chastity is adultery. It violates the marriage covenant and erodes the basic trust needed for a persevering total gift of self, one to the other. It is important that this be acknowledged as seriously sinful behavior, undermining the promised exclusive fidelity, sowing the seeds of marital breakdowns, and causing incredible harm to children.

A strong defense against these temptations is a marriage that is continually growing in physical, emotional, and spiritual intimacy. Communication and relationship skills are crucial to building such intimacy. As spouses learn to improve their communication, they can better respond to each other's need for love, acceptance, and appreciation. They deepen marital intimacy and strengthen their practice of chastity.

Gratitude

Adam's exclamation upon seeing Eve—"this one at last is bone of my bones and flesh of my flesh!" (Gn 2:23)—is one of joy. He expresses joy in receiving from God someone who is truly as human as he is, but who is different in a matching or complementary way. His joy is an expression of gratitude at receiving the gift of Eve. Eve, too, must have rejoiced upon seeing Adam, for she also saw someone who complemented her and was truly human like herself. This virtue of joyous gratitude is critical for marital and family love. Each married couple is called to foster this joyous gratitude—thankfulness that each is a gift to the other and that this gift of the other ultimately comes from God's bounteous love for them.

Within marriage the joyous gratitude is expressed, as it was for Adam and Eve, in the giving of one's whole self to the other. In joyful gratitude for his wife, a husband gives himself completely to his wife; and in gratitude for her husband, a wife gives herself completely to her husband. This joyful self-giving is specifically expressed and exemplified in sexual intercourse. As the Second Vatican Council teaches, "The acts in marriage by which the intimate and chaste union of the spouses takes place are noble and honorable; the truly human performance of these acts fosters the self-giving they signify and enriches the spouses in joy and gratitude."[90]

There is a second element to this gratitude that is related to the first. As a husband and wife are thankful for one another and express this gratitude in the giving of themselves completely to one another, so this gratitude is open to the further gifts that this self-giving literally embodies: that is, a gratitude for the possible further gift of children. Inherent within a husband's gratitude for his wife is that together with her he can beget children. Inherent within a wife's gratitude for her husband is that together with him she can conceive children. Together a husband and wife are gratefully open to the gift of children.

Marriage, then, is to be a school for nurturing gratitude for the gifts of God and for openness to the gifts of God that are proper to marriage. In practicing the virtue of gratitude and openness, spouses cooperate fully in the procreative task of married life: conceiving and educating children. Because

the children are received in gratitude and in a spirit of openness to each of them as God's gifts, they are themselves formed in that very openness and in appreciation for all of those gifts. These gifts include life itself, the dignity of human beings created in the image and likeness of God, and the wondrous gift of the whole of the earth where all of life is nurtured and supported.

Moreover, the virtue of gratitude overflows from the marriage and family to embrace the Church and the world. With gratitude for their vocation to serve, married couples and their children are motivated to participate actively, in keeping with their individual talents and charisms, in the building-up of Christ's Body, the Church.

Lastly, living a married life in joyful gratitude and openness fosters hospitality. When the spouses become one flesh, their openness makes them a home to each other. Their communion with each other becomes a home for children, including adopted and foster children. Their family, with its heightened awareness of human dignity, reaches out in hospitality to the poor and to anyone in need, in keeping with the words of the final blessing from the ritual of weddings:

> May you always bear witness to the love of God
>   in this world
> so that the afflicted and needy
> will find in you generous friends,
> and welcome you into the joys of heaven.[91]

Growth Toward Perfection

Some might object that growing in virtue—to be perfect as the Heavenly Father is perfect—is an unrealistic vision for married couples. After they are married, couples are still themselves, with all their personal faults and failings. Sacraments, each in their own way, really do configure us to the love of Christ revealed in his Passion, Death, and Resurrection (the Paschal Mystery), but they do not bring instant perfection.

In Baptism all of us are fully liberated from sin. We receive a new identity: "having become a member of the Church, the person baptized belongs no longer to himself, but to him who died and rose for us."[92] Yet our spiritual journey has only just begun in Baptism. We have to grow according to the love to which we have been configured. In Baptism we have been configured into the likeness of Christ so that we can grow in holiness of life and become increasingly conformed to his divine and resurrected likeness. We have to "become what we are."[93]

While the Church is holy because of her union with the all-holy Christ, the spotless Bride of the spotless Lamb (see Rev 22:17), she is "always in need of purification."[94] Christ loves the Church "to the end" (Jn 13:1), and he continually purifies and reforms the Church. The Church is always called to "become what she already is," the holy Bride of Christ.

In a similar way, the Sacrament of Marriage configures the spouses into a sign of Christ's loving and unbreakable communion with his Bride, the Church. In their exchange of a promise of fidelity *to the end,* their communion becomes a participation in Jesus' everlasting spousal love for his Church.[95] By symbolizing and sharing in Christ's purifying and sanctifying love for his Church, married couples are called to an ever deeper holiness of life, just as Christ calls his Church to an ever deeper holiness of life.

Getting married does not, therefore, magically confer perfection. Rather, the love to which the spouses have been configured is powerful enough to transform their whole life's journey so that it becomes a journey toward perfection. In this journey, the spouses are ever more conformed into the likeness of Christ so that they can ever more perfectly love one another as Christ loves his Church.

Marriage and the Eucharist

[The Eucharist is] the memorial of the love with which he [Christ] loved us "to the end," even to the giving of his life. In his Eucharistic presence he remains mysteriously in our midst as the one who loved us and gave himself up for us.[96]

In the Eucharist, Catholic married couples meet the one who is the source of their marriage. "In this sacrifice of the new and eternal covenant, Christian spouses encounter the source from which their own marriage covenant flows, is interiorly structured and continuously renewed."[97] Pope Benedict XVI explains how, in the Eucharist, the very meaning of marriage is transfigured: "the imagery of marriage between God and Israel is now realized in a way previously inconceivable: it had meant standing in God's presence, but now it becomes union with God through sharing in Jesus' self-gift, sharing in his body and blood."[98]

Moreover, Pope Benedict points out that the sacramental mysticism he mentions is "social in character."[99] The Eucharist "makes the Church" because "those who receive the Eucharist are united more closely to Christ. Through it Christ unites them to all the faithful in one body—the Church."[100] In the Eucharist, spouses encounter the love that animates and sustains their marriage, the love of Christ for his Church. This encounter enables them to perceive that their marriage and family are not isolated units, but rather that they are to reach out in love to the broader Church and world of which they are a living part.

Marriage continually sends the believing Catholic back again to the Eucharist. Here is where the gratitude that has become a life-giving habit in a marriage can be fully and completely expressed. "Eucharist," after all, means "thanksgiving." In the Eucharist one thanks God the Father for his supreme gift, the gift of his risen Son, who, in turn, bestows most fully the divine life and love of the Holy Spirit.

Marriage is a school for gratitude. By celebrating the Sacrament of Marriage, "Christian spouses profess their gratitude to God for the sublime gift bestowed on them of being able to live in their married and family lives the very love of God for people and that of the Lord Jesus for the Church."[101]

Procreation and education, the basic and irreplaceable service of the family to society, are part of a formation in love and a formation for love that is a participation in building up the Kingdom of God.[102] Just as the Church is a "sacrament . . . of communion with God and of the unity of the entire human race,"[103] Christian marriage and the family contribute to the unity of humanity and to humanity's communion with God.

For example, since the Eucharist "commits us to the poor,"[104] so the hospitality of Christian marriage becomes enlarged as a commitment to the "preferential option for the poor"[105] by training each family member to recognize the image of God in each other, even the least. Thus, the natural virtue of marital hospitality is nourished and formed even more widely by the spouses' Eucharistic life.

Their hospitality, in turn, will build up the Church, making the Church a more hospitable or homelike place[106] and thereby an even stronger witness to Christ's love in the world. Thus, "the Christian family [that] springs from marriage . . . is an image and a sharing in the partnership of love between Christ and the Church; it will show to all people Christ's living presence in the world and the authentic nature of the church."[107]

Marriage Fulfilled in the Kingdom of God

A marriage that is truly in Christ, a marriage upon which his school of gratitude and openness has left its mark of joy and warmth, is a sign of the Kingdom that is coming. It is a blessing to the couple, to their children, and to everyone who knows them. It offers a sign of hope and a loving witness to human dignity in a world where hope often seems absent and human dignity is often degraded. It is a sign of the Kingdom because the love of Christ moves the married couple to ever greater heights of love.

Christian married love is a preparation for eternal life. At the end of time, the love to which spouses have been called will find its completion when the entire Church is assumed into the glory of the risen Christ. Then the Church will truly be herself, for she will experience fully the self-giving love of her spouse—the Lord Jesus Christ.

This is the glorious wedding supper of the Lamb, to which the Spirit and the Bride say "Come!" (Rev 19:9, 22:17). Just as Christ once proclaimed the greatness of marriage by his presence at the wedding feast in Cana, so now, at the heavenly wedding banquet, marriage and all the blessings of the Holy Spirit, given to us by the Father through Christ, his Son, will find their ultimate consummation because we will be in perfect union with God.

A Commitment to Ministry

In November 2004, we, as the United States Conference of Catholic Bishops, made a commitment to promote, strengthen, and protect marriage. We began a National Pastoral Initiative for Marriage in order to communicate from the riches of our Catholic faith the meaning and value of marriage and to offer support and practical assistance for it to flourish both in society and in the Church.

This pastoral letter extends and enriches the work of the National Pastoral Initiative for Marriage. It is a sign of our continuing commitment and of the priority we have given to marriage in the evangelizing mission of our bishops' conference. It is an expression of our esteem for the gift of married life and love that couples share so generously for the benefit of Church and society.

The Church is built on a foundation of marriage and family life, which it cherishes as the school of a deeper humanity and a cradle of the civilization of love. For this reason, both Pope John Paul II and Pope Benedict XVI have emphasized that pastoral ministry in service of marriage and family life should be an urgent priority for the Church.

We wish to echo and reinforce that message.

The vision of married life and love that we have presented in this pastoral letter is meant to be a foundation and reference point for the many works of evangelization, catechesis, pastoral care, education, and advocacy carried on in our dioceses, parishes, schools, agencies, movements, and programs.

WE URGE a renewed commitment by the entire Catholic community to helping those called to the vocation of married life to live it faithfully, fruitfully, and joyfully.

WE PLEDGE to be a marriage-building Church, drawing strength from God's grace while using creatively the gifts and resources entrusted to us.

WE CALL for a comprehensive and collaborative ministry to marriages. Because of the complexity and challenges we face in society today, our ministry must be one that

- **Proclaims and witnesses** to the fullness of God's Revelation about the meaning and mystery of marriage
- **Accompanies and assists** people at all stages of their journey: from the early years when young people begin to learn about committed relationships to the later years of married life, and even beyond them to grieving the loss of a spouse
- **Invites and includes** the gifts of many, beginning with married couples themselves and welcoming also the service and witness offered by ordained ministers and by women and men in consecrated life
- **Encourages and utilizes** many methods and approaches in order to serve individuals and couples whose circumstances in life, whose needs, and whose preparation and readiness to receive the Church's ministry can vary widely
- **Celebrates and incorporates** the diversity of races, cultures, ethnicity, and heritage with which God enriches the world and the Church especially in our nation

Finally, **WE ACKNOWLEDGE** with respect and gratitude all those who are working to defend, promote, strengthen, heal, and reconcile marriages, either through church ministries or in other professions and fields of endeavor. **WE PLEDGE** our collaboration with all who seek to create a vibrant culture of marriage rooted in God's plan for the good of humanity.

U.S. Catholic Bishops   November 2009

Notes

1 Nuptial Blessing, *Rite of Marriage A*, no. 33, in *The Rites of the Catholic Church* (New York: Pueblo Publishing, 1976). All subsequent texts from the Rite of Marriage refer to this edition.

2 Nuptial Blessing, *Rite of Marriage B*, no. 120.

3 See Pope John Paul II, *On the Family* (*Familiaris Consortio* [FC]) (Washington, DC: United States Conference of Catholic Bishops [USCCB], 1982), no. 75: "The future of the world and of the church passes through the family." See also FC, no. 86.

4 FC, no. 3.

5 Pope Benedict XVI, *Charity in Truth* (*Caritas in Veritate*) (Washington, DC: USCCB, 2009), no. 1.

6 See *Catechism of the Catholic Church* (2nd ed.) (CCC) (Washington, DC: Libreria Editrice Vaticana–USCCB, 2000), no. 1601; *Code of Canon Law: Latin-English Edition: New English Translation* (*Codex Iuris Canonici* [CIC]) (Washington, DC: Canon Law Society of America, 1998), cc. 1055.1, 1056-1057; *Code of Canons of the Eastern Churches: New English Translation* (*Codex Canonum Ecclesiarum Orientalum* [CCEO]) (Washington, DC: Canon Law Society of America, 2001), c. 776 §§1, 3, and c. 817.

7 Second Vatican Council, *Constitution on the Church in the Modern World* (*Gaudium et Spes* [GS]), no. 48, in *Vatican Council II: The Basic Sixteen Documents*, ed. Austin Flannery (Northport, NY: Costello Publishing, 1996). All subsequent citations of Vatican II documents refer to this edition.

8 CIC, cc. 1056, 1134, 1141; CCEO, cc. 776 §3, 853.

9 GS, no. 49.

10 Pope John Paul II, *On the Dignity and Vocation of Women* (*Mulieris Dignitatem* [MD]) (Washington, DC: USCCB, 1998), no. 7.

11 MD, no. 7.

12 See GS, no. 48.

13 See Pope John Paul II, General Audience, May 30, 1984.

14 See GS, no. 48: "Authentic married love is caught up into divine love."

15 GS, no. 48; see CCC, no. 1652.

16 GS, no. 50; see CCC, no. 1652.

17 CCC, no. 2363.

18 CCC, no. 2363.

19 Pope Paul VI, *On the Regulation of Birth* (*Humanae Vitae* [HV]), no. 9, *www.vatican. va/holy_father/paul_vi/encyclicals/documents/ hf_p-vi_enc_25071968_humanae-vitae_en.html*.

20 CCC, no. 2363.

21 CCC, no. 1604.

22 HV, no. 12; CCC, no. 2366.

23 See, for example, Pope John Paul II, General Audiences, January 5 and 26, 1983.

24 See FC, no. 32; see also CCC, no. 2370.

25 USCCB, *Married Love and the Gift of Life* (Washington, DC: USCCB, 2006), 17.

26 HV, no. 13.

27 HV, nos. 18 and 23, quoting Pope John XXIII, *On Christianity and Social Progress* (*Mater et Magistra*), 1961.

28 HV, no. 10.

29 HV, no. 13.

30 See FC, no. 3.

31 See USCCB, *Between Man and Woman: Questions and Answers About Marriage and Same-Sex Unions* (Washington, DC: USCCB, 2003).

32 Congregation for the Doctrine of the Faith, *Considerations Regarding Proposals to Give Legal Recognition to Unions Between Homosexual Persons* (2003), no. 8, *www. vatican.va/roman_curia/congregations/cfaith/documents/ rc_con_cfaith_doc_20030731_homosexual-unions_en.html*.

33 CCC, no. 2358.

34 CCC, no. 2347.

35 CCC, no. 2357.

36 CCC, no. 2384.

37 USCCB, *United States Catholic Catechism for Adults* (Washington, DC: USCCB, 2006), 287.

38 See USCCB, *When I Call for Help: A Pastoral Response to Domestic Violence Against Women* (Washington, DC: USCCB, 2002), 11.

39 See David Popenoe and Barbara Dafoe Whitehead, "Should We Live Together?" (2002), *marriage.rutgers.edu/ publicat.htm*.

40 *United States Catholic Catechism for Adults*, 410.

41 See Pontifical Council for the Family, *Family, Marriage, and "De Facto" Unions* (Washington, DC: USCCB, 2001), no. 25.

42 See *Family, Marriage, and "De Facto" Unions*, no. 25.

43 *Family, Marriage, and "De Facto" Unions*, no. 26.

44 See Institute for American Values, "Why Marriage Matters: Twenty-Six Conclusions from the Social Sciences," *www.americanvalues.org/html/r-wmm.html*.

45 See GS, no. 47.

46 CCC, no. 2207.

47 CCC, no. 1607, alluding to Gn 1:28, 2:22, 3:12, and 3:16-19.

48 See CIC, c. 849; CCEO, c. 675 §1.

49 See CIC, c. 1055 §1; CCEO, c. 776 §2. A valid marriage between any two validly baptized Christians, whether Catholic or not, is a sacrament. This includes marriages between a Catholic and a non-Catholic Christian, whether Orthodox or Protestant, although certain canonical requirements must be fulfilled for these marriages to be valid. A marriage between a Christian and an unbaptized person is still valid as a natural marriage, but is not a sacrament. Here, too, for a Catholic to enter such a marriage validly, certain canonical requirements must be fulfilled.

50 GS, no. 48.

51 CCC, no. 1617.

52 GS, no. 48.

53 See CCC, no. 1623; CIC, cc. 1055, 1057, 1108; CCEO, cc. 776, 817, 828.

54 GS, no. 48.

55 CCC, no. 1642.

56 CCC, no. 1534.

57 See MD, no. 24.

58 CCC, no. 234.

59 CCC, no. 1702.

60 CCC, no. 1878.

61 FC, no. 18.

62 CCC, no. 2205.

63 Thomas Aquinas, *Summa Theologiae*, I, q. 93, art. 3, in *Fathers of the English Dominican Province* (New York: Benziger Brothers, 1947).

64 CCC, no. 2205.

65 CCC, no. 1655.

66 CCC, no. 1656.

67 See Vatican Council II, *Dogmatic Constitution on the Church* (*Lumen Gentium* [LG]), no. 11.

68 FC, no. 21.

69 See CIC, c. 844; Pontifical Council for Promoting Christian Unity, *Directory for the Application of Principles and Norms on Ecumenism* (Washington, DC: USCCB, 1993), nos. 125, 131.

70 See LG, no. 11.

71 See CIC, cc. 226 §2, 774 §2, 793, 867 §1, 1125 1°; CCEO, cc. 618, 627, 686 §1, 814 1°.

72 CCC, no. 1657.

73 See CIC, c. 844; *Directory for the Application of Principles and Norms on Ecumenism*, nos. 125, 131.

74 USCCB, *Follow the Way of Love: A Pastoral Message to Families* (Washington, DC: USCCB, 1993), 11.

75 FC, no. 78.

76 CIC, c. 1125, 2°.

77 CIC, c. 1125.

78 CCC, no. 1604.

79 CCC, no. 1604.

80 LG, no. 11; see CIC, c. 210; CCEO, c. 13.

81 See FC, no. 66.

82 GS, no. 47.

83 See CIC, c. 1108; CCEO, c. 828.

84 See FC, no. 17.

85 FC, no. 17.

86 See CIC, c. 226 §1; CCEO, c. 407.

87 CCC, no. 2339.

88 See HV, no. 9.

89 GS, no. 49.

90 GS, no. 49.

91 *Rite of Marriage A*, no. 125.

92 CCC, no. 1269; see 1 Cor 6:19, 2 Cor 5:15.

93 FC, no. 17.

94 CCC, no. 827.

95 See FC, no. 20.

96 CCC, no. 1380.

97 FC, no. 57.

98 Pope Benedict XVI, *God Is Love* (*Deus Caritas Est* [DCE]) (Washington, DC: USCCB, 2006), no. 13.

99 DCE, no. 14.

100 CCC, no. 1396.

101 FC, no. 56.

102 FC, no. 50.

103 LG, no. 1.

104 CCC, no. 1397.

105 FC, nos. 47, 64.

106 FC, no. 64.

107 GS, no. 48.